ELEMENTAL
NATURES

PREVIOUS BOOKS

Poetry

HOMECOMINGS
TRANSFORMATIONS
SEASONS OF DEFIANCE
HUMAN/NATURE
BECOMING HUMAN
WRESTLING WITH THE ANGEL

Plays

TIME'S UP AND OTHER PLAYS
TIME'S UP
FOX, HOUND & HUNTRESS
    in Vol. 10, PLAYWRIGHTS FOR TOMORROW

Novels

SECOND CHANCES

Non-Fiction

THE DEATH AND LIFE OF DRAMA
    reflections on writing and human nature
ON THE WATERFRONT
    (essays: contributor)
A POETICS FOR SCREENWRITERS
THE UNDERSTRUCTURE OF WRITING FOR FILM
    AND TELEVISION
    (WITH BEN BRADY)

PRAISE FOR PREVIOUS BOOKS

True to his beliefs, in this volume the poet creatively describes the familiar in ways that make us stop and take note. In the end, "we make what meaning we can." Optimistically, it can spring from faith, love, or reason. There is a maturation, acceptance, culmination to this book that makes it fine.

Phil Wagner on *Homecomings* (US)

Lance Lee is claiming his place in the galaxy of world poetry, grafting his work not only onto Dante, but in "River of Flesh", onto a more recent precursor, Wystan Auden. This darkly visionary poem bears comparison with its famous model, "The Shield of Achilles". He is staking out the ground of his ambition — and what is exhilarating in this work is its ambition.

Donald Gardner on *Transformations* (UK)

Unashamedly post-Keatsian in tone, transatlantic in bias, Lee's strongest strain of originality lies in his marrying of lyric celebration with precise imagistic clarity; there's the Hughsian fascination with animal forms, both real and metaphorical; there's the packed line, the lush diction, the muted experimentation and the force of a restlessness that sustains its tempo.

Tim Liardet on *Seasons of Defiance* (UK)

One of the most passionate documents of the masculine heart around. A rare book: while the poet continually hungers, the poems consistently nourish, uncompromising and very beautiful.

Pamela Stewart on *Human/Nature* (US)

This poetry is addressed elementally to its title theme — becoming (and remaining) human. It is poetry unabashed by sensuality and feeling, by declaring authorship of them, by setting 'beauty' as the prima materia of the work of poetry, by insisting on the profound and writing it large and with intensity. It is poetry that is untroubled by sincerity versus concealment and irony. It is poetry that is disconcerting — not a modern voice but rather a voice beyond epoch and cultural baggage yet rooted in his territory of that most modern place, Los Angeles.

Judy Gahagan on *Becoming Human* (UK)

A book filled with wondrous language, passion, and attention. Pablo Neruda wrote that poetry must be like bread, that nourishing and fundamental, that necessary. When I say that Lance Lee's poems are like bread, it is the highest compliment I can give.

Sheryl St. Germain on *Wrestling With The Angel* (US)

Portrait by Ron Sandford

ELEMENTAL NATURES

selected lyrics, sequences, and artwork
including the modern classic
NO ONE COMES FOR PENELOPE—
with new poems
HEARTSONGS
and the essay
THE AMERICAN VOICE

LANCE LEE

ELEMENTAL NATURES
SELECTED LYRICS, SEQUENCES AND ARTWORK,
INCLUDING THE MODERN CLASSIC, NO ONE COMES
FOR PENELOPE— , WITH NEW POEMS, HEARTSONGS,
AND THE ESSAY, THE AMERICAN VOICE

iUniverse books may be ordered through booksellers or by contacting:

iUniverse
1663 Liberty Drive
Bloomington, IN 47403
www.iuniverse.com
1-800-Authors (1-800-288-4677)

Because of the dynamic nature of the Internet, any web addresses or links contained in this book may have changed since publication and may no longer be valid. The views expressed in this work are solely those of the author and do not necessarily reflect the views of the publisher, and the publisher hereby disclaims any responsibility for them.

Cover Photograph by Lance Lee
Front B&W Portrait: Ron Sandford
End Portrait in B&W (originally color): John Robertson
Interior art as credited in the "Contents" and individual poems by:
 Michael Foreman
 Ron Sandford
 Charles Shearer

ISBN: 978-1-5320-9829-1 (sc)
ISBN: 978-1-5320-9831-4 (hc)
ISBN: 978-1-5320-9830-7 (e)

Library of Congress Control Number: 2020905685

Print information available on the last page.

iUniverse rev. date: 09/14/2020

The world today is sick to its thin blood for lack of elemental things, for fire before the hands, for water welling from the earth, for air, for the dear earth itself underfoot.

...Henry Beston, *The Outermost House*

...I wished to ... front only the essential facts of life, and see if I could not learn what it had to teach and not, when I came to die, discover that I had not lived.

...Henry Thoreau, *Walden*

CONTENTS

from HUMAN/NATURE   2006

from SEASONS OF DEFIANCE   2010

SELECTED SEQUENCES

from **BECOMING HUMAN**   2001 *selected artwork* by Charles Shearer

HEARTSONGS: new poems   2020

ESSAY   2005

ACKNOWLEDGMENTS FOR HEARTSONGS

Ashes	*Chiron Review* (US)
Kali	*Iconoclast* (US)
Report From The Front; Autumn Choice	*Ink, Sweat and Tears* (UK)
The Oranges Of Guimaraes; Red In Tooth And Claw	*The New European* (UK)
Slackwater; What Cannot Be Escaped	*Orbis* (UK)
Letter From The Land Of The Lotus Eaters; Marigolds; Nightride, Thunder, Heartroll, Stars Over The White Horse Of Uffington; Hare; This Is All; The Red-Tailed Hawk Of My Forgetting	*Pennine Platform* (UK)
Letter From The Land Of The Lotus Eaters; Autumn Choice; Red In Tooth And Claw; Nightride, Thunder, Heartroll, Stars Over The White Horse Of Uffington; Transformations; Crows In The Persimmon Tree Of Paradise	*POEM* (US)
Hare	*Streetlight* (US)
Runes; Report From The Front; The Red-Tailed Hawk Of My Forgetting; Grandfather Daddy Wilds, Or: Myth, Malevolence, Truth	*Writing Disorder* (US)

PREFACE

To be at a point in life when a 'selected' makes sense is sobering and simultaneously delightful from revisiting old favorites and other poems I feel I have neglected. But trying to pick a representative group as I'm sure many other poets have realized is like trying to pick between children. Worse, many poems inevitably have been omitted, with an added layer of difficulty here in having to pass over so much of the artwork a variety of artists generously created for many of these. I hope those illustrations included will tease the reader into getting hold of *Transformations* which gathers all the poetry with accompanying artwork together, except for that created by Ron Sandford for "An Incendiary Ground: Encounters with Greece" in *Homecomings*.

A portrait by that artist is included here too, drawn one warm afternoon in Martin Bax's home in Highgate, London as I sat in his favorite chair, shifting my position and ending up with three hands… Martin was then the editor of *Ambit*, both at an original peak and generous to me. The portrait at the end is by John Robertson for a local reading in my hometown in Pacific Palisades, a part of Los Angeles, after *Becoming Human* was published. That portrait became the cover for *Human/Nature*.

I know a reader will want some statement of purpose for such a lifetime's undertaking, but I can think of few memorable prefaces. Happily I refer you to the essay at the end of this book, "The American Voice", which gives a good idea of what I think is the real nature of American poetry. I leave it to the reader to try and fit me in there as he or she sees fit. But let me add too that it has always been my goal to be clear, and direct, however often I may have missed those goals, or despite how special knowledge of some of the historic and mythical figures treated in these pages might be helpful. Where I feel that to be the case I include brief explanations. I believe a poetry that seeks obscurity, depends on academic interpretations, or is unwilling to confront a reader's experience directly, fails its calling. No amount of obscurity or artfulness can hide emptiness, though it is also true no amount of plain speaking can make up for a lack of artistry. Poetry is always performing on a tightrope, balancing verbal force and beauty with the urgency that drives a man or woman to speak to others in this manner.

The title, *Elemental Natures*, reflects these concerns. If I am rooted in the most modern of cities, Los Angeles, as some have noted, I am equally rooted in the natural world around me whether in California, New England, where I was raised, or in England, where half my family lives. But these have always been the starting points for a poem's journey toward what is as essential and fundamental to another as for myself. That is as true when I give voice to historical figures, or animals, or reimagine myths in modern guise. Our lives are bound together. We constantly mix self and other, just as the present mixes with the past and any number of hoped-for futures. Under the unrelenting revolutionary changes through which we are living, in a world grown as volatile, dangerous, and as strange, this journey towards one another, the burden of the lyric 'I' of these poems, has never been more important.

Poetry's mansion has many rooms, far more than we have explored, any number of which we now no longer enter or have forgotten. Time is the only critic worth paying attention to, and time itself has lapses of memory and unexpected recalls. So what these poems achieve remains largely to be judged, celebrated, forgotten, or rediscovered as that judge wills. For now I am content if they give pleasure to old friends, and bring me closer to new.

for Jeanne   as always

LYRICS

CLICHES

Don't write about roses or dawns
   two hundred years after Keats:
of how waves gut themselves on the shore
   as pebbles choke in their throats,
or sunsets sputter in storm

   under slabs of slate-like clouds.
Night is not Death crowned with stars
   nor the dark mother, Peace,
who bore us into this world and waits
   to collect us, after:

Spring stirs with hope, or none—
   Nature is mere nature—
put these clichés aside, the children
   of our cultural youth, torn
hackneyed, not worth mending.

   Be modern, urban, talk of terror,
bombs, disease, race, war, rape,
   debate who is at fault, and rage
against the abuse of children:
   talk of how change carries us on

its shoulder so fast into the future
   we are dazed and turn with
desperate force to godlets for answers
   however often they go down
in suicidal throes or up in flames.

But should we close our minds
to how we offer our cliches
    father to son, mother to daughter
in a relay race without beginning or end
    to lend, we hope, some grace?

for nature is not jaded—
    there are only cruel or worn out men.
The sun rises out of a tight-fisted dark
    a violent rose of fiery petals,
their sunset red intense from the night

    dawn does not chase but swallow.
Clouds of thorns with shining tips
    drive wedges between sky and earth
and like nails driven into our flesh
    wake us from lifelong nightmare

so we cry out surprised we are alive,
    borne on a surge of power
out of ourselves to find the world
    pure marvel
and all we thought so tired

vivid and vital as blood in our heart.

TURTLE & ELEPHANT

Three years dying...
"Oh God!" Grandmother cries
just after midnight when her mind
stumbles to a lucid moment.
She just turned 88 and remembered

to brag: now
the end.
Her iron turtle that lifts its shell
when a foot steps on its head
is in the hallway; her elephant

stands minus one ivory tusk
on her old, heavy dresser, animals
kept for luck:
they, with De Haviland china, Sheraton chairs
grouped around the white

formica-topped table, and lacquered
red chinese coffee-tables
are all that's left. And Mother
faithful at her side, unlike my childhood
when Grandmother always nursed me

happy to be sick and home from school,
waiting for Mother to blow into my room, a
"Here I am!" a kiss a gift a smile
then only her fragrance left
to mix with the hot rags

fried in fat
Grandmother pressed to my chest.
Now her final breath...
Mother holds the old mouth shut
until it stays.

Three years Mother nursed like this, doing
what she couldn't,
transformed
though she wonders
when they wheel Grandmother out

and later when her ashes
join the Pacific
so what? and thinks, better a
"Here I am!" and the rest
at a swift end.

We are spared nothing. Now
the turtle's hollow closes
around her and
from the dead woman's room,
the maimed silence of the elephant.

HAWK FOREVER IN MID-DIVE

Autumn dogwood and oak clutch their yellowed
    billet-doux like the old woman in her
attic, surrounded by her attar
    of decay. Leave her alone with her heart's
wooden tissue. She will come downstairs soon
    to escape the late heat, go out
to her covered porch and fan herself
    while hawks bank overhead or stoop
on their prey, fanned like coals by the air.
    She steps on old copperhead on her walk—
he gives half a twist and the barest
    flash of his fangs, just as one did to
my daughter years ago. Grandmother wounded
    him with stones until I took his head off
with a shovel. She was vigorous, then.
    Now she edges away to her lilacs—
their flowers were spring's. Seven kinds
    of apples grew from her apple tree once,
including one plain tart green one she called
    "Mercy" and used for Thanksgiving.
Her feet on the patio are leaves blown
    over flagstones. Aimed at her head,
beak thrust out wings angled severely
    a hawk hangs frozen in mid-air,
fanned to permanent fire in her sky.

WHAT SHE TAKES FROM ME

We argue in the house like a change of seasons—
when I am Schumann going mad she says
    "Here's lithium, be composed and silent"
or Van Gogh removing my ear
    "Here's white paint and grey dawns"
or Duchamp with my chess
    "Here's the local bus map and help-wanted ads"

so I come outside in this steady downpour
and stake myself in freshly turned earth
    beside tomatoes and strawberries,
pummeled peas wild on the ground
    with profuse snap-dragonish blooms.
My feet become thick roots,
my hands a foliage of cradling berries,
my eyes green fruit
    that dawn through horizons of dark, bitter
        loquat leaves.
Soon waxwings with ember-tipped wings
will forage through these,
children pluck the peas from their pods,
and herself, with a laugh, lift her dress
and belly with picked fruit.

BACKRUB

She leans forward, clothes fallen to her waist,
my hands stroking down to the twice-broken bone
    at the spine's base,
slipping lower to the lobed softnesses I knead
    with wide fingers, then up
to where they cut her cancer out,
tracing that footlong scar over her shoulder
    towards her breasts:
no matter how I rub, that length of white stays
    white, dead white
when blood runs in our lovemaking.
She murmurs and turns in my arms, brushing aside
    her hair
with its coppery highlights, encircling me in turn,
    open, everything offered
these many years. I can't stop rubbing
as we make one body, share one scar, rubbing
at that long white question, that death
as near to us as skin.

NIGHTSHIFTS, AUGUST RAIN, LOS ANGELES

Rain grumbles in the run-off, tired from the long flight
    from Mexico.
I listen for leaks,
to the cat beg entry like a child,
the dog pad back and forth and need a curse to settle down.
How can the woman sleep cool to my touch
while rain chokes in the run-off, then floods over the half-
    dead avocado's roots?
I think of tearing things out,
of new jobs, women, pets, poems,
of how I've lost years from my life
until a stranger stares at me from the dark with my eyes—
"You can never know," he murmurs, "you can only lose."

My mind spins with replies, the wind
with flares of rain

    then
    I am the rain
    falling
    falling.
    Starved trees
    grow new arms
    flower-laden
    at my touch;
    the woman
    looks in eyes
    so familiar, so strange
    she melts
    beneath me. Now
    I give and

give and
give
I forget
how tired I am,
how far I have come.

RECOVERY: EVENING STAR

Just before midnight...
The caved-in wreck holds our daughter—
she weeps her blood, red beams
wheel over her face:

the jaws of life cut her out
while we still sleep...
Then, awake, we make one bitter honey
hived in her bright hospital cell

until, months later, she recovers.
Now I've come here to rediscover
how sun shines on a beach, or from
a seal's flank on sea-drenched rock:

how it dwells on blue pinafores
lupine wears in the near field
and glows on the cow feeding her calf
to be food in turn. Now I know

how blood waters the earth,
how flesh is food and death
sits always to a banquet— I still see
my daughter's free leg thresh the air,

her heartbeats race past two hundred
to the minute until the nurses,
tired of alarms, turn the alarm off.
She never knew when coma swallowed her,

how her brain nearly was siphoned down
her spinal chord; she never saw herself
gnaw her lower lip fat, or heard
the animal-like clatter of her mouth,

or her howls spill into other wards.
And she never saw how we were
too moved to cry when she woke up
and grew again from an infant—

in six weeks she reminted herself
from the dark press of her forgetting
until she remembered laughter...
The sun beats down, loosening

the limpet-hold of memory...
I sit until I glow with heat,
a patina for muscular stars
to rub off: until the sun sinks

through a low fogbank
and twilight opens its wings. Somewhere
a thrush sings darkness into evening
and the first star rises

bright as any I have seen,
but my heart is hard with questions
about cruelty in the heart of things
mixed with such unexpected kindness—

for though our daughter is home again
and whole, we live always in danger
of great loss and in need of
heart-wrenching gifts.

THE SILENCE

This will sound strange: for six months
silence gripped me fiercely.
I was afraid I would be so alone
I'd be dead, or that I would hurt
wife or child or friend to prove
myself alive. I found silence everywhere:
in the arms of my wife, in passion;
in work, routine, the chance flare of laughter
with a friend; under the high night fog
when the Pt. Sur Lighthouse beam
played with hill and ocean and touched me:
in twilit mountain woods as I hiked homeward
and heard an impromptu Sunday service
someone had brought his violin for: the silence
was deeper when worship stopped, heavy
as the black waters fish hunt with light,
where the deep songs lack the weight to fall;
where there is nothing at all but all
I might risk from imagination or yearning
or the rooted desire to know myself.
This was the strange thing: I feared this
naked opening to my will, this freedom
to be whatever I chose, this freedom
that shed all others, and recoiled,
though I had fallen silent to come here.
I sit now at the dining room table, working
as my father used to work, all others forbidden
to come near, as I was forbidden, though
they are all nearby: I think this repetition
of what we have known is all there is
of bulwark and meaning and measure,
though this is less than a melody in late woods.

Now I type: "Who am I?" Now I ask aloud
"What is my life for?" without fear,
without fear of an answer all silence.

PARTINGTON RIDGE

When I raced up that canyon
blind to wash-out and slide
my shouts filled the folds
where redwoods clung to echoes
of winter's floods, and went through
oak groves loud enough to silence jays.
What did I shout? Enough.
I wanted justice that day but found
its stub-end in my hand by choice.
I looked back at the Pacific
simmered under a falling flame,
some brown lichens of houses
by the coast road, and damned
myself. Jays spindled shade
up and down the hill's swift slur
where I stood half in the light, half out:
a rotten log at my feet pointed down
the gorge. I jabbed loose bark,
bared grubs who called this fallen thing
home, broke
into the empty defenseless hole:
from full height full-armed full
of my strength
                    smashed my stick down
and threw the stub-end after the sluice
of rotten lumps and maggots
until some downslope redwoods
dammed it all in their roots.
I heard silence, a squirrel whistling
as he whisked his broom down an oak,
a hawk, water
in the gorge's throat
all vowels. I heard

silence. I heard silence
under my breath's near surf
all around, always there, sane
as arms curled around a child.
I never knew how I settled
past mustard I had snapped
and heavy-headed milkweed,
a cloud of calm. I found myself
in creeksplit redwoods and followed
the water to the cliff
where it jumped out of itself...
A stray far crow moved across the sky...
I had to remind myself what I had heard,
but what was that? The low sun
took my shadow far up the canyon
where the hilltops still sweated,
half in the light, half out, all warm.

SOLITARY, IN STONY FIELDS

The door flaps its dead limb,
a black room
begs entrance:
high wind comes flickering down
    through the snow:
is anyone home?

This sifts through me
as though I were wide, empty spaces
where mockery could echo
and query and silence
set stone walls to mark fields,
this here, this there,
this mine, this yours

for we were here
we built these walls
in wide fields secure against
    all comers,
living wisely, living alone

until we trespassed against
    each other.
We built new walls then,
stone by stone between us
the closer we grew.
Love grew better unsheltered,
beset.

We finished like vines
hung around a dead tree
that threw bare limbs
through our cloying, clinging green:
sweetness can kill.
This death at least we knew,
this life feared more

this life feared more
so clung to the dead core.
High wind, sift my snow.
Door-flapping dead season
I'll latch you shut

as an old New England shack
its lock rusted tight
its emptiness locked from the light,
solitary, in stony fields.

WHEN MELVILLE BOARDS THE ACUSHNET

his first whaler
he is twenty-two,
his hair in the breeze a wing
hammered to a masthead.
The sails belly like women.

I try to imagine him young,
sober, Dutch-American, another son
who ships out after a larger god
to strike with loving steel—

or as one of those helmeted
on their bikes, heavenly thunder
machined between their thighs—
as one of those washed up in New Delhi
holy 'om' rolling its stone
room to room in vacated hearts
like the boys go, town to town,

booming. I look all the way
down the cylinders of his eyes
to nothing.
                    No wonder he finds himself
at sea, whose eye, like his,
reflects all he doesn't have.

He pauses, now, as he rolls
towards the horizon with a limp
in his mind, and watches the land
slide its hump from sight
with a heave of long, flat flukes.

MONET

paints lilies at Giverny
while mustard gas oozes its cream
over a green canvas.

He's old, the days of his years
flocks long numbered and folded
into twilight, and now this work
with paint and brush bows
him over— lilies,
always lilies that breathe

while the dead pile up at Lille
like burst tubes of paint.

He goes on measuring
the light across the lilies
the colors in the light
the colors he dreams the lilies dream

with the richness
of the richness of fields strewn with the dead
when the green comes up
the following spring.

He knows how we go on in our lovers' dreams
after we have gone, shimmering
from the black unconscious like lilies
rooting beauty in decay:
he goes on

from love for the young men sown
in fusillades across the fields more bountifully
than seed. Stroke

by stroke
across the endless canvas he
bears them to another life.

A CHORDAL ECSTASY

1

He discovered, as if new
the intervals of the chords.
His heart gave a sinuous flash
past his net of ribs.
Here
was the key to play himself
the world.

He made hooked eels of trees,
toes root like anemones,
houses cut a crablike choral dance
down the suburban shore:

he reshaped the ocean into a net—
no fisherman or waterskier or oceanic tourist
escaped his unfathomable haul.

2

He seemed
with his white hair
that disappeared in the sky on gray,
   luminescent days

a baited hook, dangled
from another world.

It wasn't long before we,
fruit smashed in our ears, our eyes,

a black drool of seeds down our cheeks,

came for him.

3

We taught him, laboriously, silence,
how no one loves to change,
how to die is our only charge.

We took the upheaving world from his mouth
we took his mouth

we came for his head and hollowed it out
like a melon in season.

4

Why, then, dose he
fin into my dreams?

His tongue swollen as a loaf of bread
with unspeakable song,

those intervals of the chords
schools of fish he cannot tooth,

that deep writhing silence from which all song
strikes?

OPOSSUM'S DEATH AND WHAT HAPPENS AFTER

His low, white seeming-clot of a body
moves fluid as well-kneaded meat
as he comes to the meadow, though the stars'
teeth shine and the night's tall weight
presses him to the ground. His snout
swings his body back and forth
as he smells how other bodies smell
distinctly as meadowsweet or rue,
and so solidly they are almost there:
smells how wetly fear threads in the air
he rolls on his tongue until drunk
and full enough of courage he goes
after the mouse or rat that unspools fear
like that. Hunger starts its blade-dance
in his belly: his teeth grind in anticipation:
he's so absorbed he never sees his danger
until claws rake him to the bone. And though
he swings around and puts his whole body
into his bite until the stranger's blood
runs in his fur with his own, he's hurt.
He lurches for cover, his teeth rattling
in that dark. And there there is nothing
he can do but lie down in his body
and die in perfect anonymity.

But sometimes he comes back,
a small question in the meadow
among the greater ones to ask,
not to smell what others of his kind
may have done in the night, or remember
how glad he was to kill or brave

24

when he fought— but because he still
smolders with a kind of amazement
at how, as he waited, death grew
from his body's own breathless knowledge
and desire.

ANIMAL POEM

There's no time to veer from his small shape
as I turn the corner: a thump, repeated,
and it's done. My rear lights show him
stand and freeze, defiant, as death pours
into his mind, blood onto the street.
He dies on his feet, snarling.

Where did he come from, slow forager, opossum,
expert in hidden ways, third one dead
this year? Around me I guess an animal life
held secret as the sleep of dreams
from fear at what we do with knowledge.

I don't stop beyond this look,
or watch, later, for his removal.
After the rains there's no trace but memory
of him rising in his dark pour,
his teeth brilliant in the light,
as if staged.

I want to wring some currency
of meaning to make good
his death or my behavior,
but there is just one less animal,
and, all around me, a secret life
grown a little poorer.

TO MAKE BREAD

you must want to work the earth, to break
your nails, to scrape the furrow clean
for seed. Sow that with wide swings
of your arms until your shoulders ache—
then wait, without trying to find a shortcut,
for winter's white yeast to puff the ground
green. Knead sunlight and water into that dough
until it turns the color of hard use,
then take a knife and cut it into weights
your back can just bear. Beat
the dough down, let it rise, mix it
with the milk from your brow and the heat
from the sheets of flame down your back
as you muscle in all the cold, all
the pain, all the hard labor you've spent
your days in; knead in the nights
when you didn't spend yourself idly
but out-waited impatience or the need
to fault others because this making bread
is harder than you thought and follows
none of the recipes you looked toward
in your innocence. There's just
a last warmth for the dough to endure,
a last rise to await with restraint,
as you might with a woman
you've never made love to before.
Now you cannot tell your crusted sweat,
your white flesh, apart from what you have made;
you are a loaf of astonishment as you understand
you are food, complete, ready at last
to come to the hands of another.

BECOMING HUMAN

The dog's tail pounds the crib's bars,
black and ominous, waking me—
or the moans do from the nearby bed
where my parents couple. Slowly
my eyes move up the wall,
but where the ceiling should enfold,
star beyond star pulls me deeply
into the night. Fear swells,
and my heart throbs— I gulp the
breathless vacuum, and thrash—
then wake, swallowing
great gulfs of air like milk.
Slowly night spins down
and topples over.... I see the terror
that fills my heart so suddenly, so often,
is just the memory dreamed here
of how I learned I was alone
and became human. That terror lies
at the root, nutriment and gnawing tooth:
it is the life I must not wake from, now.

THE WOLF

1

A wolf lived beneath the stairs:
when I ran across the living room
his breath singed my legs before
I leaped to the safety of the steps.
I was four, the year they told me
I had one mother, not two:
the year my sister was born and
bemedalled Uncle came home
and barred me from his mother's room
as father had already from mine.
I listened to Prokofiev's story
about the boy who cried wolf too often,
and thought, alone at night
despite those softnesses just down
the hall that teased my mind,
he has nothing on me
with my own wolf at my heels...

2

An early TV stood before his lair,
screening him with images.
I remember one, a white horse
at war's end, legs splayed
topsy-turvy in tattered snow,
staring back in fear like me
whenever I crossed that room...
The house felt frozen yet feral,
springing again and again
from some deep trance

as Mother, Father, Grandmother, Uncle
smiled and smiled and smiled
over girlfriends, infidelities, rivalries.
Snowy images lingered on those early TVs
from Father Knows Best, or I Remember
    Mama,
and all the other waking lies we echoed
as though the black true beast was not
the dark screen our family idyll
    glimmered on.
That was the war to me, not the
wide, slaughtered starving world.

3

Grandmother sold that house
to stop our warring masteries.
I thought then to cross rooms wide as years
    without pursuit:
that such hunger I felt, desire
turning on itself, anger
the world could never match a boy's dream
were just my childhood lot. But now
I am in the middle wood, winding
    in the trees,
hurrying through the clearings, I know
the rage desire and anger feed and form
    is not put by—
for the wolf runs in the heart:
there is nowhere to hide.

THE GHOST

billows in full sunlight beside
the overturned chaise-lounge, feet floating
over the lawn, rainsoaked rhododendron
blooms glimpsed through her dress
as purple stains. I guess

she's my young grandmother or
my mother's loose-haired loose-
clothed dream of herself one summer day
before her life settled in
come to judge me— or

my middle-aged hunger for beauty
come to taunt with what cannot be.
I'm hungry for her to forgive me
but when I read my strangeness
in her eyes, I feel

a stone settle on my shoulders
for each compromised year and know
she is the measure of my fading.
She leaves like a photo brightening to white
I race to fill in with features

of everyone I have known— and I sense
I am wrong, that she would let all of us
touch the blood of our births
to lip and tongue and again
be young, if she could. I float

over the damp grass after her like a double
exposure looking to merge with its original
until harsh with this giddiness
I pull back to the first moment
I saw her so troubled to be seen by me:

she knew then I would follow
no better angel into a second life
but locked in stubborn flesh and decay,
inevitably betray what all men do:
life, love, eternal youth.

OUR GREAT LONELINESS

Sweet Rosemary, fresh as new snow,
white skin ablush from fun as we played
on the top bunk... Not children, not teens,
we kept our eyes on the game though I
saw the clean line of her thighs
her skirt half hid, and felt such desire
I saw myself push the game aside
and cover her face with kisses,
then cover her as a man a woman,
cries of ecstasy filling my ears.
I thought she must see, and recoil,
but she played on, oblivious, or pretended
to see and feel nothing of my wild want...
I felt alone, and untrue, and ached.

I return to this moment often—
a silver brooch still holds her hair,
and her scent envelops me as we bend
our heads so our breathing blends,
yet never, then or later, more... Always
I wonder at our silence, and feel
manhood and childhood begin to part
as the first mature touch of that great
loneliness a man and woman shares,
brushes my heart.

BATS

I have been troubled by bad dreams,
so when twilight floods out of things
into darkness, and my face appears
in the window when I turn on the light,
I study its broad, high cheekbones
that make the flesh photograph heavier
than it is, the straight gentile nose,
brown eyes that stare straight out, head
held high: brown hair the sun burns blonde
from the celt and german in my blood;
the familiar, ironic twist of lips.
Not much suggests the ghettos of Kiev
or Polish Vilna my father's fathers left,
or why any from those left behind
should crowd into my dreams
with my face, my pipe, book, beercan,
wallet photos, loose change in their hands
from the mass graves and lime
they must have gone into, holding air...
Their history is divorced from mine.
They never came here. They are divorced
by my father's family's rush
from Garchmarski to Levy, now Lee,
divorced once my father let my mother
raise me anglican, not jewish.
When father's father heard of that he shouted:
"Are you a mouse or a man?" at his son,
yet when grandfather died I found
Hebrew prayers for the dead
on my father's bureau: he never said them
that we could hear. 'Remember
those who were lovely in their lives

whether they were killed, slain, slaughtered
burned, drowned, or strangled:
ask for their names in your blood:
blood remembers' I say, now,
though words never saved anyone,
though I cannot imagine being
led out to a hot dissolving dark...
The wind soughs through the trees—

> *I look in the mirror— I am twenty*
> *years older than I thought. I stand up,*
> *stretch my legs, strange from the coma*
> *that held me. I walk down a street*
> *and push a Jew into the gutter:*
> *he bobs, he cringes, he snaps one look*
> *at my well-dressed pitiless shape— .*

My head snaps out of sleep. I am sore
and sweating and turn the light off.
My face vanishes. I open the window
on the night, and the wind comes in.
We always think we'll do the right thing.
Outside bats hunt down the helpless
with their sharp, black wefts of song.
I slide downwind with them, violent and small.

RUNNING WITH THOREAU

Strange hungers drive him
through Walden's oaks and pines
after vole or fox or deer,
longing to gulp hot blood
and still fluent muscle,

face red, eyes shining
even as ferocity pulls him
to all fours, then to his belly
where he twists side to side
and coils, hissing.

At first light he finds
his cabin door and crosses
the threshold, shaken, human.
Later he floats on the pond
feeling disembodied as his face

stares back from the surface
mingled with clouds,
for he knows now
what thrives in the blood
is "sensuous" and "reptile".

I know him well
in this land where I
listen to coyotes sing
on the near ridge at night
and imagine them hunting

through dense growth—
then hear Thoreau
running in the canyon woods
and slide beside him,
my snout tugged forward

as I topple to my paws,
canines thrusting from my jaw,
symphonies of spoors
growing vivid on my tongue
as we hunt swiftly over

the forest's rotting floor.
That feral nature I
always knew was mine
overwhelms my heart—
until I find a familiar door

and hesitate, listening
on the threshold
for my wife's breathing inside.
I remember how it was
when children lived here,

and how we made love
when they slept, laughing
as we swallowed our cries.
I straighten to full height,
wondering

why our hands
are not all stained red
by the animal we are.
Nights pass, months, years
as the answer grows,

yet even now when
blood cries for blood,
I barely know how to guard
the small exchanges of love
that make me a man.

THE LIGHT AT VEZELAY

This light pours pure as clear water
through La Madeleine's plain windows,
laving the woman's relics who loved
too well yet was greeted first by Christ
when he returned from hell.

Once knights jumbled downhill
colorful as tumbled tourist curios
as St. Bernard called for a new crusade:
when they roared consent,
birds fell from flight, stunned.

Now we enjoy pastoral views,
then stop for tea and pastries, girls
in starched aprons, no one about
this Sunday in November but us
as sunset flushes walls and roofs

deeply as ingénues with lovers.
But I cannot kneel and pray
in this sore and dreamless time
however I feel the old hunger
for something better in my heart,

for this light falls always on hungry flesh
and world-weary pilgrim, saint, and
soldier cutting his way to victory
with a prayer: even now, somewhere,
it imbues the blood of innocents

with a bright, deranging beauty.

A GRAY WIND IN NANTUCKET

All last night the gray wind blew
from Madaket past moor and Sconset bluffs
into the steep Atlantic: blew
past this high room only a step from cloud
and the road where wind always blows
and so seems always in the same place,
restless as me. Moments ago
our lovecries floated outside
just as captain and maidservants'
fell with the lightness of scented pollen
from a high room of our friends' house
across the way long years ago.
No one disturbed them then, or us, now,
though that captain's wife listened
for the lovers' footsteps to descend.
She said nothing when they appeared,
to preserve their lie: now she haunts
    the wooden passageways,
no more able to rest than old harpoon and
    hook in the attic
who dream of green sea pastures turned red
from whale-bread sliced at its harvest.
That grey wind blew as our friends
shared family woes, always so unique
    and so alike,
born from love from truth from kin
who do what they must which we must endure
with a growing knowledge of evil, the gray wind
    knows,
blow by blow.
           Our curtains hang still:
the slow front that pummeled our thin roof

and woke me early, sags eastward.
Light so drenches the room
only kindnesses seem possible.
I don't know what our friends will do,
but love, turn to me again here, for we are in
some grace of tide and sun-shattered storm,
free to fill these moments with our joy
before the gray wind returns
and we too must wait,
like that listening wife, caught
in some enduring knot of yearning,
for lost happiness.

.

GEESE

Daily they practice flights of Vs
these buoy shaped birds
who soon must fly south.
The sky whitens with the season,
frost burns the tundra gold and red:

one day ice shines through noon
and hearts harden to the gauntlet
they must fly— ozone-free light
that irradiates and warps the gene,
acid rain that burns the feather,

and stinging air from great cities
that makes them fly blind. Storms
roll them into airy heaps, and guns
wink from estuary and pond
where they think to rest

until the beloved's wings go limp
and plummet to waiting teeth
happy to sink into grief. Only then
do the warm waters of their refuges
embrace and solace them

as they fall from the sky like confetti.
Are they so dumb or so forgetful
they come and come again each year
never changing their way?
Or from some well of fellow-feeling

do they forgive without demure
the death we bring as the one
the world exacts for life?
How innocent they are of our denials,
our artilleries of self-hatred and despair

that turn outward and become bullet and gun.
The sun shimmers from spread wings,
their cries and scribbles crowd the sky—
then they are gone, as though erased,
a last feather spiraling down

through the silencing, haunted air.

WHAT GOD DOES WITH OWLS

Have you seen an owl die? Or
are they the true immortals, feeding
on the carelessness of others?
Maybe their bodies incandesce
at the moment of death
like a camera's white flash...

Does God give them then a place
on the tree of life, in heaven, never
to hunt the small shapes at its base?
Or does He put them in
some dark corner of His mind
where every hunt succeeds,

meat a hot, perfect red,
nights full of small scurryings,
thuds, sudden cut-off screams?
And does He who is everywhere
loose Himself through the air
in them too, talons out-stretched,

deal the deadly blow, tear a cry
with his yellow beak, stretch out
his head to let warm flesh slide
down his maw, enthralled
while a heart still beats in His claws?
What does He do with owls?

Surely not condemn them for doing
what He made them for?
I think they are closer to His heart
than us, like all wild things, because
they are perfect in their wills,
in their griefs, their pleasures—

not cross-grained with defiance
like ourselves, careworn, at a loss
to make sense of Him, or our lives.
It is us He puts in some dark corner
so we cannot infect these others
with our wear, and doubt, and wonder.

AN OLD BARN IN WESTON

stands in a field of dandelions blooming
so intensely the sky steals their hue.
A few tools rust, abandoned; the lofts sag,
barely able to support their emptiness,
and the barren stalls lose even the memory
of horse and cow or crowing barnyard fowl.
Homes fill once wheat-rich fields,
bound by law to look older than they are:
metal snakes commute down Lyons Plains Road
each morning, and each evening, home:
by day lonely women lug their wetnosed young
chore to chore or, chauffeurs by night,
drive young couples date to date
who all but couple in the backseat dark.
No matter. A trunk weathered white holds
the barn gates closed: heat warps the walls
that ice cracks in turn. If time speeded
the stained brown walls would hurry inward
under the falling roof, groaning with relief.
No one comes here now except barn mouse
and field, who was always here, and,
ghosting on wide wings as twilight falls,
great white mouse-harrowing owls.

ANGELS

His death is so new blood smokes into the colored air
    the screen places in my living room.
A woman bends over him, arms thrown wide then folded
    over her breast,
repeating all the crucial gestures of those medieval figures
painted at the foot of Christ's cross as the body descends.

Younger, I watched the city burn while I lounged in a pool,
only later learning Watts was smoking picturesquely
    in the distance.
I felt divorced from my own distress.
Now I become the woman and kneel by the curb,

a babble of Spanish grief on my lips:
I crane past the police cordon, too,
                    an onlooker eating
blood and lamentation. Only moments ago
the gun trembled in my hands like a woman in ecstasy.
The soul can be anything

a life grows into its care.
Being human is an ideal, something akin to a painted
    angel on blue or gold
just out of reach of earthly hands.
I shut the image off and the screen, luminous and virginal,
dims slowly into the darkness where I am.

BORDER CROSSING

On the beach south of Ensenada
the pelican-threaded surf
through wavecrash and foamrun
and the groaning suck home says
"nothing nothing, nothing:"

Far to the north at Big Sur the same
white words. Between these Mexicans
stand on a wave of land in Tijuana,
reduced to silhouettes by brutal
border lights— they look like trees

after a fire has swept them,
hoping to slip in a confused
moment into that brilliant land.
I feel their hunger as I pass, the
commonplace heartlessness

of men set against men,
the pity in my heart that leads
to nothing but waste blood,
a black thread in the dark red.
There are friends to think of,

the drug of easy pleasures:
I put these others from mind
until the surf takes on urgency
when the house sleeps. Then
I see them stripped by desire

to outlines of humanity, men
who want what they cannot have
and despise what they do. Men
like me. Mile after mile the
white words tumble on the beach.

DACHAU

I pour over maps in flight to a wedding
until, just north of Munich, I see Dachau.
History is a dream in Los Angeles, but there
I could stroll barracks and ovens as though
    on any Sunday outing.

Both German and Jew stir in my heart—
when my fathers abandoned history for America
    a century and more ago,
they left whole families behind to devour each other:
perhaps one forbear casually flipped the switch
    releasing gas,
while another shipped in from Kiev or Vilna
    beat the air and cried
as the showerheads shook and hissed...

The same skill in killing turns now towards
    ruthless comfort:
if, tired, I fell in Munich's new airport, a bed
placed just so after careful calculation
    would break my fall,
while the roads south steer the car as though
    trapped within a map.
Then a surprise— pastoral as Iowa, green
    as Vermont,
the air a familiar, humid flood,
the landscape brings no comfort but tells me
even here I am less a stranger than I thought.

In Italy as my daughter treads the aisle amid
    our jubilation,
and her child wails, full of new life, I go on
    awakening to Dachau's life—
and how both killer and sufferer root equally
    in my blood.

THE QUAKER GRAVEYARD IN NANTUCKET

They baffle me, these non-violent men
who still heave harpoons in their dreams
at peaceful islands of flesh, then stitch
through ribs with long spears until
they stab the heart and spumes of blood
rain on their sober grey, man and whale
wallowing in a sea stained red.
Still they flench flail slice hook drop
the whale's flesh in boiling pots,
refining all anguish and triumph
to an oil they sell at premium prices
to other men they never would harm
or help. Their wives beside them dream
of store openings, of cash and flow
to mark the days before, oil-smeared and reeking,
their men come home to spawn in them,
and later in their maids: such ecstasies
rained from attic rooms and cupolas...

When these Quakers gathered in church,
they struck through silence to God,
spearing Him with such passion
man and woman sweated tears
that ran down their cheeks, so transported
they changed sorrow and pain to delight,
and evil, grained in the world like quartz
in softer stone, to clay.
                    They knew
right turns wrong with the flip of a fluke,
that the heart is flat deep cut whole rank
lustrous.
                    So they forgave Friend Owen Chase

who ate his men to survive the long row
to Chile after the whale sank the Essex,
not a make-believe Ahab but one of their own
who found the human and inhuman
lie close in a man's heart.

Night opens and closes overhead;
thunder and unrolling, strobe-lit silks
trail eastward over the waters:
stars tirelessly dry the darkness.
The Quakers sheathe their spears
and guide grave ships over swells
I cannot see, their wives patient
as when fog rolled in morning and night,
so fused with sunlight they were blinded,
and thought the strange hard husbands
forming before them were black,
imagined shapes. Now, a jet-ride away
the grave Pacific rolls over
wreck and tooth-scored bone:
nearer, hasty, the careless Atlantic
bares a keel on a sunken bank,
then covers both once more— while in town
all have forgotten how a hand may slice
an innocent heart, yet still caress so
even reluctant knees buckle and fold...

Let me not feel small beside these men,
ashamed at the gentle mercy lavished on my life
that finds no evil without repair
or grief without recovery.
Let me not grieve for murder at sea
or lust by land, or the hard inner light
that holds all conflict within one sphere
and sees true—
                        for my innocence slips
under their wake as a whale's stripped body,
cut loose from the head, drifts down
to the depths where evil abides, and courage,
and lust, and the sea's violent peace....

WHY THE WOMAN LIGHTHOUSE KEEPER STAYS AT POINT PINOS

1

The light burning into the dying
eyes of sailors as they go down
to their drenched holocaust, cursing,
lives in the tower's tooth behind the beach
where the beast of the foghorn lows all night.
When my children call from their dreams
in fear of the wet ship of the ocean
with its dreadful cargo
I soothe them with lies:
    "Hush, darling, you hear nothing" or
    "No, no darling, there is nothing to see"
for the drowned men are bells,
and ring among the sunken ships;
the drowned men are lights
and shine in the depths
where hunters angle their own bright flesh
    for prey.
Some nights, when the moon wears a shroud
they pool together in phosphorescent schools—
the fishermen know when they spill
nothing from their drenched nets—
only the mesh gleams
until rinsed again in the sea.

2

One calm, clouded night I went to the shore
the wind still, and the waves,

even the foghorn, broken:
only the light turning and turning behind me

like meat on a spit
swept over the sea

as though beckoning.
The small lights of the drowned converged

until a broad beam lapped the shore—
when I touched that brilliance,

it clothed me, I shone
as though on fire.

> they said *We are changed, not dead*
> *though dead to you, moving*
> *steadily in the sea's steep currents.*
> *We hate your heat, the terrible*
> *briefness of your purpose;*
> *hate the living heave of*
> *your belly and the greedy thirst*
> *of your thighs; hate*
> *that light behind you*
> *rolling horizons together, as if worlds*
> *and time and hunger were cheap*
> *and they are.*
>   *Come, be*
> *distilled to us—*
>   *all that holds us*
> *even this close to life is your grief.*
> *We hate that most.*

3

When at length I fall asleep
near my children who rest
like infants on the breast

once primal fear has worn them down
and peace curls and settles
on their brows,

I know something bred in the bone
hates life
and even then is eager to be free.

That hatred is our mystery,
something we must teach to forgive and remember
that we may live despite our pain.

So you will find my spirit here,
mourning,
as anyone must who loves,

long after the point is stripped
of cypress and pine to fuel
the local fires. Hear me

in the sea lions' roars,
in the foghorn and ocean breaking
on land and rock in wind and fog—

or see me, though all slips away
and so much so willingly,
in that great wheel of light

rolling our darkness home.

THE SOUTH SUSSEX DOWNS

for John Matthews

Everywhere the ancestral mind—
field, windbreak, barrow, altar: on the crests
warriors and horses etched in chalk
refuse to go away, like bad dreams.
Everywhere the ancestral wind, blue and silver—
Mary's colors, the mother the pilgrims loved
who once traced this road through Alfriston,
then abandoned with the dreams in chalk.
Light wheels across the shore-hugging sea:
rain falls with a thousand years' despair
and the downs hood their heads with dark mists

and then the amazing thing
the land takes itself back from us

swallowing every human sign except
the drunken will-o-the-wisp villages
that stumble in their muddy troughs.
"Can you feel the brooding?" asks my friend,
yes! I want to say, but I can't shake the terror
gripping my throat and then, huge,
the exhilaration:

> *as though*
> *I rise from a trance on the hill, set free*
> *by the land's freedom, made fully human*
> *only by passing through.*

ANNIVERSARY CARD

They dazzled rooms they entered,
one dark, one blond, together all
we mean by beauty. My father bragged
of his beauty queen queen of New York
models, this icon to be envied.
But even then he was unfaithful
with some singer, an affair fanned
by his mother who hated mine,
     'that shiksa'.
Phone calls were monitored, letters
steamed open, a detective hired
to undo father's lies— yet after this
I found mother in his lap in glad tears.
Were they each other's forbidden fruit?
Did they love their own beauty,
seeing themselves in each other's eyes?
Or were they just two young lovers love
lifted past their faults for love's season?
When did love stop being enough?
To think, in Venice, she returned
fatigue to ardor, or much later
reduced him to prodding pillows
     and brushes
assembled to mime herself in bed
in the separate room where she slept,
asking:
     My dear, is it you?
to find she had fled with his bankbooks.

Yet for forty years they exchanged
a new year's greeting, a rite continued
even when he remarried. At last
she kept the card, ending even
the *deja vu* love's memory had become
with a final, puzzled shrug.

HOTEL-DIEU, NOVEMBER

The fields lie fallow... White rows
of stakes mark endless graveyards
that green and burst in season.
Yellow and purple chrysanthemums
stream from high windows, and blackbirds
swarm the fretted steeples as though

five hundred years of tending
the sick and poor have not ended.
But the Sisters who cared have gone—
only tourists like myself come now,
and buyers of the vineyards' pick
who gather here each fall.

My heart is like this place,
fallow and ripe, caring and grown
calculating, so that I recall youth
as these halls history, to find
something better than this present
coldly mature air. Yet sometimes

when warmth wells up from depths
where hardy blackbirds never fail to sing,
I cease to envy those loved poor, and feel,
surprised, a grace like one of their
vanished Sisters move through me,
ministering solace hurt by hurt.

Beaune, Burgundy

PLAYS WITHIN PLAYS

Strange, this sky— a fin of fire cruises westward:
   naphtha beams— flame throwers in an
      otherworldly war—
boil the clouds and choke the light:
   Vs of geese, and lower, a cloud of crows
      fly swiftly through the murk.
Another moment, and the sky transforms
   to gold tissues, some lamé, and darkens
      by stages to navy, glittering strands
as though a dancer shedding veils.
   A last orange flutter of coals,
      and night draws a curtain over the field.
Who is watching? I wonder, chilled
   suddenly sure all this is a show
      for an audience behind the sky
for whom even now I am part of the play,
   the hero in the dark.
      Who sees me for what I am?
Am I anyone at all?
   Or am I married to a role called 'myself'
      that turns out instead to be all mask?
I scurry from the field,
   confused by the doubts
      the black hawk of anxiety
lives to slide down the wind and strike.
   I hesitate at my door:
      love, and light, are there, and those
who will give me a name and place, pleased
   I am home,
      wondering what kept me—

how can I share my fears
  and make their happiness insecure?
    I go in quietly,
answering smile with smile.

BUDDHA IN LOS ANGELES

I wanted to live deep and seek out
the marrow of life.... Thoreau, *Walden*

Where is there peace? where death
as black beaks tear ripe persimmons
above a fallen glory of orange leaves?
Already narcissus blooms and violets
purple green shadows in this hot now
cold now summer now winter air.
I feel surreal as images jumbled on film,
unsure who I am, or when. I burst
in white flames from the tips of irises,
sink mineral by mineral to bulbs
with greedy lips, and nourish a secret root
as rain falls aromatic and sweet
from high eucalyptus leaves where
fog's cold streamlets tangle and grow thick.
I'm wrong wanting to island myself
from this flood— even silence fills with
my blood singing, while sleep becomes
another waking. And though my heart
calls anything but its own eternity *the end,*
death only changes one life to another,
here. No one can escape. All I can do is
                    live deeper.

WHY JEFFERS STILL BUILDS TOR TOWER

an elegy after Robinson Jeffers

Five years Jeffers wrestles stones uphill to Hawk Tower
in brilliant light or gray, burned or soaked and
chilled by the heavy-shouldered heave of winter surf
roaring on the granite shore he quarries.
Muscles clench and loosen, grow hard as quartz,
    fluid as wave:
                    when he pauses,
he stares into storm and finds God in its heart, still
building this world as he his tower.

Done, he prowls the tower's rampart,
driven to poems heavy with granite's old fire,
and the waves' long heave, winter light, and chance warmth,
each enough for itself, like men are in God's eyes,
one called forth for his good, another for his wrong
as surely as day alternates with night
however we call ourselves free.

Years pass like ships on the horizon.
He loses love and, bitter, wrestles death to a draw
in hard supple songs that make his conflicts our own—

even now from Hawk Tower in kelp-sharpened air,
as a seal coughs rounding the point in calm, summer waves,
and light swells out of the west that here turns east,
infusing all with a crimson glow that unstrings the will,
he labors on his ramp, back arched as a drawn bow,

muscles working like water over a reef as he rolls his life uphill,
for no tower, however high hands dipped in sweat and granite
   and song may build
can bind the restless and unmoving
or reach that place where peace abides, and be done.

HARRY'S PLACE AT HAMPTON COURT PALACE

Catherine screams in the raven gloom
whom Harry loved, and every Tudor Tom and...
She was a true Tudor rose who knew one season only:
 ever-opening.

Harry cut off her head.

Greater Wolsey sighs where recent fire
bared his stuffy gilded study,
throat so dry sandpaper in the sun is damper.

He lost everything to Harry over another skirt—

only death cheated Harry of his doom.
Why do they stay when they could ride belief
clear of our flesh instead of watching me, now,
 with no soul to lament

walk through their old rooms in January?

Imagine how Catherine felt before condemned,
a pure fragrance in impassioned air
touching every hand, held by none:

or Wolsey, more surely feared

in the company of his peers than the tomb:
and how his throat muscles strangled him
at the end, and Catherine

woke to reality when the crowd roared

as falling steel sliced her neck:
what surprise   what bitterness to discover
they weren't immune from our plain state.

Who would not have stayed reproaching Harry?

Brutal, conscience-clear, faithless rhyming Harry
who led them through these gardens,
savoring the freshly severed head

of the winter sun swelling on the horizon.

HANNIBAL /AT SIXTY

First mites attacked, all those hovels
between royal guestrooms whose faded gilt
Roman threats expelled me from—
    killing them
takes forever. Next a tooth chipped,
Expensive, unseen, an Egyptian sighed,
his fingers under my tongue
    Let it go:
at your age all recoveries are partial,
the lost parts of the body become
omens of the soul's fate. That winter
    a cold brought
gum ulcers: a Babylonian in a slum
did nothing, too— they left
reluctant as lovers to part.
    My knee buckled
next— *You're worn,* a Greek Hippocrates
said: *something in your knee has torn,*
you'll heal, but always have a gimp.
    I thought of battles
I survived hardly scathed, no wound
worse than a hook in my thumb
instead of a fish when nine—
    or was I ten?
How far behind is death, eager
to plant us in time and place,
when we lose the dates of our pain?
    Better to have died

at Zama, the Roman death machine
all swords all javelins all my long lines
bared by my own cavalry:
  to have died the
Martyred Hero of a lost Cause,
not gone from thick king to king
urging they fight before the Romans
  picked the gold
from their heads and teeth. Now
I let them find me by this shepherd's hut.
The archers circle—
  they come no closer—
they still fear me, when the future
is what tears all that matters from a man.
Their arrows nock and release—
  find me oh Death
a feathered heap in tufts of sheep's wool
and dusty, beetle-riven dung,
bald, old, absurd, spared.

ACTAEON

*Great was the chase with the hounds for the
unattainable meaning of the world.*
                        Czeslaw Milosz, *"Winter"*

Actaeon's fingers are spring leaves
    in a light breeze on lyre-strings, the
        outward echo of how a surgeon touches
the heart's web of arteries and veins.
    The lord and lady, warriors, dogs, servants,
        the roar of flames in the hall still
as he noses a spoor of song to the story's lair
    where a man half animal waits,
        or heroes clash sword to shield,
or a woman and her lover thrash
    where her angry mate enmeshes them.
        None stir: what loss   triumph   shame
defines a life that echoes their own?

He leaves them late,
    the flare of truth replaced
        by twined flesh and lovecries.
Black streets, a simple room, old maidservant,
    bread and water, payment tossed aside—
        he wants another gold.
His pupils come at first light, slight boys
    to teens whose shoulders thicken
        who chafe to be men, lethal and heroic,
bulls with girls.
    But Actaeon leads them like wild horses
        around and around a corral

with a rope of fables.
    This world he says *is a story*
        waiting to have its meaning laid bare.
Listen— and listen: look, and look until
    the breeze becomes words, the shudder
        of leaves, flesh, the river murmur,
dialogue, stone a Yea! or Nay!

They leave aroused, the commonplace
    given a mysterious sheen.
        On impulse he calls his old hound,
back bent like a bow,
    and walks under the noon blaze
        the same white as the streets
where so many hide behind their walls, wise
    to avoid being caught in some moment
        life writes in red,
to be instead the audience stories feed.

He reaches the forest where even shade is hot.
    The hound laps water from the stream
        like a machine.
Actaeon edges along the bank as though
    tracking some scent to its source.
        When the waters grow wide and calm
a small stream courses off.
    Something as light as spring leaves
        in a light breeze
touches his neck and makes his hair rise:
    he whirls— no one— someone—
        something

he senses that does not act
　　but watches without pity or cruelty,
　　　amused, sad, will-less.
The hound's hair ridges down his back.
　　　　　　　　　　　　　　Come
　　he commands, choosing the unknown way.
　　　The beast follows,
back straightened, a snarl gleaming in his eyes.

Actaeon finds himself hurrying until
　　branch-whipped, thorn-torn,
　　　his breath a curlew's whistle,
his heart a roar of waves, he falls
　　against the hard *No* of the earth
　　　and jams moss muskily into his mouth.
When he looks up, the grotto.
　　A small rivulet arches over a cliff, the
　　　movement of sun on water spring leaves
in a light breeze.

　　She is there,
　　　flesh flawless.

He gapes, and stands carelessly, staring.

　　Their eyes meet *and he understands…*

　　　She is a young girl on her bridal bed,
the shy husband,
　　their tremble, penetration, joy:
　　　and She is a sword raised high,
its perfect edge,
　　a stream of blood blurring its sheen,
　　　a head rolling on the ground;

boys who give grace its meaning
   as they arch and ache
      against one another in the gymnasium;
the smoke of incense, of crematoria,
   bitter flesh driven unwilling to the fire,
      the fire;
the choking dust across the battlefield,
   the blind men, thrusts, wounds,
      the flowers around their graves,
the spring leaves, the light breeze;
   the newborn's howl,
      its mother's smile,
the birth blood wiped from a new face;
   the whitecaps on the sea, the sea,
      the wave that swallows men in their boats,
the swallowed men,
   the fish that gnaw them bone white,
      the bones:
and the grieving heart that begins again,
   that risks love to find love—
      and love's betrayal.
She lets all wounds be forgotten
   and tirelessly gnaws the heart's red bone,
      bringing all to perfection,
kind or cruel, Her beauty
   the only mold,
      the truth at the end and beginning
of every story.

Actaeon does not reflect
   A man must do what he can,
       and beyond that be content
—no, he has found what he wants
   and screams, and runs
       runs as though horns grow from his head
and an animal bellow pours from his throat,
   as though hounds leap to the chase,
       as though he is the hounds and the hunted,
the teeth, the torn flesh,
   the terror, bright blood
       and the final heartful, heart-rending
horror, and delight.

EURYDICE

My blood sings to his words
    because they give me myself;
I love his hair tousled over his brow
    or combed back, bouffant: love
how he flings his clothes on or off,
    his belly a touch too rounded,
his cheeks smooth or unshaven,
    his long-fingered hands on me
deer in a forest, sometimes certain,
    sometimes all flight. I love even
his unwashed machismo:
    I am all flowing scales and sudden
plucked ecstasies. Why, today
    he made silence sing, dancing
before a great heron—
    the wary bird was entranced
by his body's music, and I,
    and the sea, who stilled her waves.

But he lives only for crests—
    when I want to wash clothes,
comb hair, shave cheeks,
    listen to another's song grow in me
he goes mad— *Me me me* sounds
    behind every word,
each restless shift of arm and leg:
    he turns from rain on dry land
to rain on floods, snow
    on snowdrifts, sleet on ice.
I become his levee, plow, salt,
    anything to contain, order, melt:

it doesn't matter what face mirrors mine—
   I am because I change.
Slowly, as he before the heron
   I learn a new word, and leave.

He turns to animals who love purely—
   birds who perch on his shoulders,
snakes uncoiling from the hollow
   of his emptiness, dogs
panting under hand, lions
   who sleep with lambs.
He craves God in a crystal, love
   in a string tuned high 'C', all
but moaning *I can't get no*
   can't get no   no satisfaction though
he never sings another's lyrics.
   There is always pain enough,
why add more? I think, and return.
   You are in hell I say, giving words
to him now: *follow me— I will lead*
   you out if you obey…
He fawns at my heels…
   We seem in a tunnel
with light ahead, or in the light
   with darkness swelling…
My genius, he murmurs, *transforms*.
   I start to believe this time
this time   this time   but I see
   he thinks only 'humor the woman,
lead by seeming to obey.'
   I stare him from sight.

Later, he lies— I hear
  in that hell we share
from fear sharing is a dream
  and we are locked in ourselves,
that love is the illusion
  which lets us bear our loneliness.
Perhaps it doesn't matter—
  someone always wants more
than he can have, someone's heart
  is broken, another's mended,
someone stays in hell,
  another moves on.

I am surrounded by children
  and presumptions I humor
from the one true virtue, kindness.
  The music here is sparse
yet beautiful because all there is:
  I no longer live in the poverty
of its hope to be more.

REMBRANDT TALKS ABOUT HIS WOMEN TO ME

"What stick arms jut beside swollen breasts
    that sag on flabby mounds
while thighs flood wide as smaller women.
    I saw how far we can fall from grace
until only fit to roll naked
    down a dirty street.
Even my wife swells under her robes,
    but red-lipped, swollen cheeked and
candy fleshed, breasts heaped and stomach
    ready to be bared, pressed, licked,
squeezed sucked in measure to how much
    I wanted to eat beauty.
                        Forget the portraits—
they paid to be seen like that
    though even those lack your worship
of thinness even when it maims.
    Maybe I was careless to measure women
by warring waves of hate
    or lust for life unending—
I was full of myself, godlike, young.
    But look at you in your Cafe—
a woman hacks beside you,
    smoke burns your eyes and grays the air
like a low fog over a field,
    and music throbs in your temples
as you flip through my gallery of extremes,
    straining to understand,
your soul wracked with hunger.
    Yet you were careless of beauty too
until your wife grew a scar back to breast

Art by Michael Foreman

and wrote "we die" in your heart: until
a daughter cut from steel lay unconscious,
    her brain swelling like forgotten fruit
in a cupboard, while you ate and ate
    to bury death under ham haunch arms
and thighs— with that madness
    you must understand mine!
Later, my wife dead young, son frail,
    few commissions, passed by by style,
bankrupted, disrupted, desire
    a girl's clothes torn by a maddened mob,
I saw life is little and easily harmed as flesh,
    though that is tougher than the soul it sheathes,
the hidden fire any draft blows out.
    I dissolved my silks and brocades
into rough brush strokes, knife smears,
    finger moldings over the bareness
nothing clothes long,
    and married desire's dream to disease
that martyrs even the corrupt,
    and to water's tremble because
someone I loved made it tremble, because
    love trembles from knowledge of its end.
Where I lie is cold as a rasp on ice.
    Your Cafe is sickroom stuffy.
Day disappears into its rags and blankets.
    The waitress hurries as if 'to be' is 'to rush,'
as it is. And now?
                    Say with me:
    'I am done denying the truth is plain,
a lit window to walk towards
    where someone I love waits for me
to grow old with her if only
    I will come in from the false dream

there is anything about us to waste.
   I am become water, and tremble
from my love's least touch.
   I am become the hurt of desire
that deepens with time and makes
      simple things most precious to hold.'"

STONEHENGE IN WINTER

These stones are never lonely in winter,
nested in grass always green:
even now brown fields are plowed and seeded,
furrows blackened with feasting crows.

Why, the gardens along the roads from town
are full of winter cabbage and chard—
heads of lettuce burst from the ground
and fill the air with green balloons.

These bluestones and grays
are battered seeds left from a larger time
when the land was still unwon, the soil
not fueled by falling generations

now so fused with earth and mind
the engendering root defies all cold,
and fans its veins as deeply in our hearts. Love,
let us make through this demi-winter's afternoon

what the land makes in its hidden fever,
and when we tire, rest in each other
like these stones on the earth's green breast,
whose milk is forever spilling over.

COYOTE

New worlds open to me,
steep stone hives that scratch
the night sky littered with light
like dank alleys with drunks
    and food;
and suburban lawns
where children play,
staring at me, amazed—
for I have run the gauntlet
of gun and trap, felt poison
eat through my gut, the earth
reach overhead and the womb
spill me out reborn before
I had time to forget or despair.
I go where I choose—
only shores I never saw before
stop me, waves breaking so unlike
those Pacific waters I knew.
Evenings I gather with my kin
and yip and yowl on
the metal reeds of our throats
such spirals of sound my fur
ridges down my own spine.
Then she comes, crying with
the crying I must sate,
my back arched into a bow,
head arrowed over the ground,
slavering, pent with the promise
to fulfill— and I do— ah, love,
    I do.
Then, at last, peace. And
just past the edge of sound—

in the darkness— darkness itself
singing my song, singing
survival, passage, passion,
    triumph.

THE WILLET SOARS

I walk my sore back straight
   down the winter shore where
      tall waves lift, their crests slurries
of wind-whipped foam, hard
   winter sand trembling like a woman
      nearing ecstasy
as white explosions roll down the bay.
   The headline roar dims in my mind,
      and the endless want of the common day
in which I drown.
                    Nearby a willet
   lifts his head—
                    I quicken my pace
      to trap him between the waves'
onrush and my path, focused on
   the now, here— he freezes
      as water rises up his legs, then leaps
into the air with staccato thrusts
   of barred wings and skims the
      shoreward foam to fade, I think,
into the gray, but instead banks sharply
   over a tall wave and soars in a curve
      that takes my breath away.
                              My heart
follows his arterial throb of flight
   into a spinning world of windsilks
      sliding through flared feathers
like water pouring through fingers
   to pool at our feet on uprushing ground.
      Later, when I feel my soreness again,

and again those lives near me
   define my own for better, for worse,
      some part of me goes on repeating
that soar and swoon earthward, animal
   merged with animal, care surprised
     by elemental joy.

AUTUMN, TOURIST, FATE

Sea and sky are blended gray.
Gulls, sandpipers, terns afraid to fly stormblind
   ribbon the seaweed-littered shore—
      a restless flutter as I near,
and their ribbon lifts overhead and settles
   in my wake. *Always* a tourist,
      inland I note the rich smell of woods
silvered with moisture, how roses still bloom
   and the great hydrangea flowerballs
      wait to don winter drab,
each season the former's dream.
   A place that makes me see this deeply
      should be home, but the sawbuzz and
hammerclang of men sealing summer homes
   send me to join the migratory crawl
      to starless cities. There I avoid
the great rhythm of life and death
   without which love has no depth
      although I trawl those streets for all I leave here:
a man's fate is to find and lose
   what must be found and held.

HOMECOMING

I am caught in the hall of mirrors husband and wife become,
bound to the urban streetweb where only earthquakes
   remind us the world is real
and far beyond disliking does not care about us at all.
I go down to the gray shore and plunge my hands in wet sand,
feel the cold saltrush on my feet, bruise my flesh on quartz
   quarried from foam;
or rub the smooth boles of eucalyptus on the cliff,
the rough flesh of oaks who weather heat and cold but not our
   acid air,
crush an earth of seeds, bark, stone, leaves, soil in my hands,
breathe in the sweet, acrid smell of chaparral fog pushes
   grudgingly uphill,
but none of these return me to myself.
Then the familiar Red-tail that haunts these cliffs
whooshes by so close I meet his eye—

> *now I circle*
>   *lazily upward where the sun burns my back,*
>   *then swoop down a precipice of air, claws fanned out,*
>   *death dealing but past guilt, free of humanity.*
>   *My small figure stands rapt on the cliff,*
>   *no more than a tree or stone or deer.*

At home I see my furniture, clothes, paintings, woman's smile,
    waiting embrace
with a hawk's sharp eyes, stunned by her giving despite the
    massive, amoral fact of the world.
No hawk, not a killer, not guiltless, I let her touch make me
    a man, her love make me real.
Here is my ocean, fog, light; my stone, my earth, my self,
    my flight.

KILLER BEES

wing north from Mexico tirelessly
   stinging their foes to death
      and living to kill the next.
They give death a face of swarming
   pain, they make death a thing of
      wings and a lethal hum as though
honey bees feasting in flowering plums:
   or stand in for the stinging years
      that make us draw the grave overhead
for relief. I discolor maps, charting
   their sweep north.
                      They will not pass me.
   I hold a fiery smoking torch in one hand,
poison spray in the other—
                   I'll swat and
   batter those that survive with this page,
      hurl downpours of words against them
splash ink in their eyes and, at the end,
   bite and snap off their heads
      like shrimp.
Not that death will care once here:
   he will fly out of my mouth, flutter
      in my veins, throb in my heart,
make my body his hive.
   Well... Better to fight just bees.
      Let the little bastards come!

A THUNDERCLOUD ON A HILL IN MAINE

I saw a thundercloud lean on a near, steep hill:
   when it rolled downwards I bolted south
      with my loved ones
as it came on faster than I thought possible,
   swallowing its brilliances.
Each time I wake, my heart pounding, to chase
   pre-dawn hauntings from their corners
      and late feasts around the dining table
   as the fog eats the stars
I am startled how the little I know now
is so much less than the little I knew young.
Near and far, nature and man, you and I mix
   so profoundly at that hour
I cannot tell one from another, but fill
   with sadness at love's infinite daring
      yet limited power to have and to hold.
I know past argument how you and I will go,
   not with a bang or whimper
but in the embrace of that storm I glimpsed
   muscled with lightning on a hill in Maine
      beating in the blood,
turning the mind to ash.

ARMAGEDDON

Great galleons move across the sky, their sails bellying high
    while their keels
cleave the blue, our lives below strange as those in coral reefs.
They see how blood stains the earth or rivers run red where
    our races meet, our dead
fish laid out in open stalls, eyes staring; or asparagus spears

laid shoulder to shoulder, ready to be bagged; or scattered
    tomatoes dismembered
and smashed; or red autumn leaves that swirl downriver
towards some sea... From these you can see history boil, a
    school spinning on its axis
deluded safety is in numbers as jaws rise from the deep

and beaks splinter the air to spear into their midst.
    No wonder they stay overhead, as we do above
scorpion fish or electric eels pendant from their caves.
They sail on... The sky gleams a blue concave, a telescope
    to study innocent and abused,
child woman man abused by child woman man

drunken doped fanatic jealous greedy vengeful taught
    to kill with a cherub's smile
or face broken from lost love, lined flesh pulled down
by grief, fists lashing out or worse, visiting their fate on
    those coming next,
passion governing all. No one comes from any heaven

we can name: no one speaks to us now. We are alone.
    We are what we make.
Another line of ships draws near, their keels black beneath
storm-gray canvas: lightning forks down, and a thunder
    too distant for sound
makes the air tremble...
                    Soon, soon they will be here.

RAVEN, AS LOVER

Eat my ears, my hair, eat
my eyes   cheeks   nose, eat
my throat, the slick tunnels
for breath for food: eat the
nape of my neck where you
nuzzle, arms that embrace
you, legs tangled with yours:
body   liver   kidneys   heart
eat them all, spine   nerves
breath   lungs. Eat my dreams,
thoughts that wake me
at four a.m., and those
that make me me. Eat my care
coldness   dead sleep   turmoil.
Eat me all, triumph   defeat,
infancy   old age, all the pain,
hope gained   lost, between.
Eat the space my body fills,
the memory of that space,
my mothers' songs that lulled
my cries, my father's absence
that made me want and hate
at once: eat what I have been
with what I am. Eat when I
betrayed you, sang or wrote
songs and poems to others,
came home late or lied or
loved badly, drunken, asleep
before done, snoring: eat
all that too. Eat my kiss   caress
joyous thrust   release   seed
jetting blindly, my spine's

ecstatic shudders. Eat my
future. I love you so much
you can even eat my death
and let me live forever.

WILLIAM JAMES TO A FRIEND IN TRINITY CHURCH, BOSTON

"Cool your face on altar stones, let halleluias
    rob your mind of thought—
        however my heart yearns for more
than the death this world couples with life,
    even more it hates to be deceived.
        I knock on the iron door, ask the indifferent
dead to answer, and when their silence and
    early morning waves of dread boil my bile
        weigh varieties of faith,
but will not blur into that mind I sense watching—
    passive—   silent—   everywhere—
        some life force or, likelier, outward division
of self I greet as a stranger, not God, unless one
    still to cut his teeth   stand   learn to talk.
        Better to fan myself in Boston's humid air,
admit men   women   children are broken
    by blows   swords   bullets   bombs;
        by lies that eat the heart, like
all is well, we suffer because allowed freedom
    yet God remains the way   the light   our deep relief
        eternal life   unlimited power,
void of responsibility— no:
    if He is as things are, we are better off alone.
        There is no excuse for just one innocent abused.

Earth   wind   fire   water and those other elements—
    flesh   blood   bone   nerve with its pent lightning:
        hunger   yearning   weakness   strength
that is never enough: rock gleaming when wet,
    water beading on the edge of singed leaves,
        a newborn's cry one floor below where others

routinely die— these are our truths
　　however we tunnel in the heart after the infinite
　　　like miners after a rumor of gold.
God, if anything, is the life and death we live."

REVEREND JOHN THOMAS

Where are you, John Thomas,
              who left suburban ease
        to minister to the urban poor
    in corrupt, dreary Bridgeport?
              I felt God, I told him before I was confirmed,
    felt the burden of belief,
        felt time was a flight of stairs
                  to travel up and down
      to speak to the famous dead.
        The other teens laughed,

but he knew my sense of history was a quest
                  for meaning and shape.
        How could he know
    my father's name was absence,
              the God I felt the puritans' or prophets',
    near enough to talk to but unlike theirs
        mute. I was happy
                  when Thomas left us in midlife,
        driven by his hunger to serve.
            I imagine in another life he sculpted stone

to the same grace as a portal's saint
              in the crypt of some cathedral,
        someone I would help, smiling
    among the stonechips
              in a barely lit place
    where tourists never come.
        Look— chisel and hammer in hand
                  we perfect a design in stone
if only for ourselves
              in love with love's ideal

which has no unlit places to be uncaring
         second-rate, hurried;
      where the thing is done for its own sake,
   without compromise—
         for what is given for love
   is given well in all ways,
      even if the faith is a dream
      and love, God knows,
      has more betrayals
         than the stars, numbers.

Only a poor light glows where I pause
         beside my friend
      to brush chips and sweat from my face
   as we shape ourselves,
         blow by blow.

HURRYING TOWARDS DARIEN

Then felt I like some watcher of the skies
When a new planet swims into his ken.... Keats

Where am I hurrying in this London
   of gasoline and diesel fumes eeling
past stalls of molding greens, where
   bloody smells from butcher shops
mix with fishmongers' scales and guts?
   No hearts break over lives in decay
behind rotting brick and eave, or when
   the too-rich earth of storied graveyards
reeks, or when the rich perfumes of girls
   with red, pimpled faces envelop us
as we pass the piles of rotting homeless.
   A taste of brutal centuries, of dull violence
grown inward, lies on the tongue.
   I shamble along as rain sluices the streets
until bats of light strike my shoulders
   from a black-and-blue sky. Amazed, I see
buildings transformed by a moment's sun
   into medieval-cum-modern altarpieces,
rich red-oranges in a steaming glow, as if
   like Balboa between one step and another
I find a new shore by an unknown sea,
   dazed by an undreamed magnitude.
The gray sky thickens. The glow dies.
   The dull and dying regain their mastery.
I am haunted by how renewal   redemption
   a dream of perfection   are only an

angle of vision away, and so much harder
    to find than gold in lead. Yet now as I
trudge on I search though this grime and grit
    for the Darien I know is here.

LAUGHTER

for Alyssa

"I don't know if I can do this"
my daughter, thinking of
divorce, mid-30s, unsure, words
an eery echo of my father's
as he visibly faded, as if we
can avoid what we cannot.

I tell her layered with years
is better than a teen or twenty-
something thin with experience—
each layer gives us more
to eat in a crisis. I say
when each part of her

emerged years ago from
accident and coma, tuned and
played with her ensemble,
humor came last, laughing
at all life does, even at death,
shrinking him so

his robes puddled at his feet
while his scythe slid from
his hands. Her face unfolds
from grief's crinkling to a
smile. Soon, I know, she will
look around, and laugh.

THINKING ABOUT HAWKING AND BLACK HOLES BEFORE A PORTRAIT OF A LADY BY LAWRENCE IN THE HUNTINGTON MUSEUM

The tribe gathers around the fire, eyes
    so many stars, darkness else:
and in the flame, in its heart, the dark spot
    that traps our seeing.
I hold Hawking's latest in my hand, heavy
as the universe, light as the universe,
    explaining the universe,
and toss it where flames flip its pages
before the darkness crushes it from sight.

Here on the museum wall the portrait
    of a lady,
just head and shoulders, flesh faintly flushed
    as though by passion's first stir:
the wheaten, beaten gold of her broad hat
    haloes her face
to emphasize her smooth cheeks, lips
    naturally red just parting,
no detail more, just that warming color
    as I feel her move into life,
eyes fixed on one suddenly in the room
    with us, Lawrence—

he loved her, I realize, it's in the paint—

she melts through the canvas   the wall
and floats into her own dimension,
drawing me with her sweating   wanting
her lips her waist to yield to mine,
trapped in a desire that outlives the years— .

I shake myself free before a portrait
    seamed with age,
Lawrence still and silent in his grave,
others passing by on the creaking floor,
    unmoved by what he has painted here…

Again the tribal scene…
My eyes shine among the starry throng:
some turn to outer darkness, some flash
brightly before they fall
       into the vault of absolute love
            that outlives the years.
This is the one story to write, to live,
         to get wrong,
    get right.

WALT WHITMAN COMES BACK FROM THE AFTERLIFE NEEDING

"a last leaf of grass to give my work its finis,
a hymn for the flowers that root in the buried in Rwanda,
    Srebenitza, the fields around Auschwitz   Bastogne
    Verdun,
for the cut-string puppet men, the ragdoll heaps of murdered
    women, the black children whose bellies balloon
    skyward.

Look how the shooter's brow creases as though in deep thought,
    how his eye trains along the gunsight, finger tightens on the
    trigger, shoulder jerks back as the bullet flies loose:
such effort should crown a work of grace
but a hundred years of murder show the worst and best revolve
    in a fatal dance.

I sang the soul is one until birth and each birth one word in the
    long sentence the soul speaks to the world,
not ego or self, or some fragment, an arm a breast
as though the long line my thought needs is just this word or that,
    vowels or consonants—
you sing denial, fighting over your plains   rivers
    mountains   inch by inch so the earth sloshes with
    blood—
you break apart, you atomize
                    I know

I aim
  I fire
    I fall backward from the massed machine guns over
    barbed wire:
I choke as the gas comes down in a room so full I cannot fall
  until all fall down,
I close the oven doors, I lime the bodies in their pits:
I hide bombs around my waist as you embrace your child,
I am the embrace, the child, the mother searching the littered
  street:

I fly into the tower,
  I cry in the seats,
    I leap into a gulf of air from the fire towards a hard peace,
for you and I make one I/Thou.

In quiet moments we forget what blood makes the flowers
  grow, asphodel and nightshade, rose and shy lady slipper,
  mums and hyacinth, whatever the dead once loved,
and gather them while children play and shriek under a
  fountain in summer heat.

              Look how night deepens as its petals close......
Man woman woman man man embrace, the divided body
  straining to be whole again.
I hold you, you hold me, and when our lovecries stop sleep
  teases with dreams of peace, as though trying to hum a
  melody we have forgotten.
I am that melody
  that forgetting
    that hunger to wake from death and sing."

LES CORBEAUX DE BONNIEUX

In my dream
   ravens fly a rough edge of stormcloud
      over the far ridge towards me
on a high terrace in Bonnieux.
   The wind shreds their wings so galaxies
      of feathers whip overhead:
loose grapevines thresh the grapes—
   the tall spire of the cypress
      bends low as the lavender, an old man
who groans and mutters as he tries helplessly
   to stand...
               Then the lightning starts,
     flash after flash over the cedars on that ridge,
the thunder lost in the clatter of debris,
   in the strobe-lit dance of leaf and limb,
     in the whir of desperate wings
and the wolf-howl of eaves like living things
   afraid of the looming dark.

                  I know
     I must not go under those clouds
darker than a starless night—
   I raise my hands and cry
     Stop!
Yet though the eaves still howl, shutters bang,
   old man cypress groans as he bends
     to the air's torrent,
feathers whirling overhead,
   that stormfront comes no closer...
     The tension becomes a rope tuned near breaking,
whining to the lightest touch...

Art by Charles Shearer

That tension is with me when I wake.

My mind slides down the dim hallways
of my warm, quiet house;
    down the well-lit passages and turmoils of the past
        in greater numbers than I recalled
but whose weight I now know;
    then feels towards the future until
        I sense where those rough birds
send their warnings the storm must break at last
    and swallow me...
                            After a moment of chaos,
        leaf and limb will still;
grapes hang motionless from their vines,
    the cypress rebound to its sentinel watch,
        clouds clear, the sky empty of wings...

I won't be in Bonnieux then,
    nor will I go with such drama,
        but be in bed, at home, surrounded
by those who love me,
                        or more likely
    find myself marooned in some bright dismal place,
        translated into tubes and machinery.

But I tell you that is not how a man should die.
    Treated small, we are large,
        not one of many, but unique.
A phalanx of ravens should cry out
    to make others stop what they are doing
        and attend the moment of our passage.

Then *I* will close my eyes and let those wings gather me,
  a silent lightning at last illumine
    where I must go.

    .

SUMMER'S END

Winter surf beats the shore with
   its fists, hair blown back by wind,
then steams across the beach,
   eating half summer's sand in hours.
Dowitchers and banded willets,
   curlews with bent smiles and
stabbing long-beaked godwits
   reclaim the foamy edge between
the settled and insecure. I long
   for day to crisp the air, night to weave
cold and smoke from a thousand hearths
   as heat and cold become lovers
who cannot be with, or without, each other,

   for I do not know myself in summer anymore.

Fishing boats trawl nearer shore,
   no longer picturesque but manned
by men in earnest who know how
   winter waves become steep islands
toppling from their weight, or towering
   foam that sweeps the headland
where summer tourists stood
   to admire the shore below.
I go down in myself to the forging
   fire atom, stone and marrow recall:
crouch, as though by flames in the lee of
   a dune to count the warm days left
like coins from a small, hidden hoard,

   for I do not know myself in summer anymore.

SCULPTOR

Dust on his pants, chips at his feet
　　time chisels my woman's face.
First her features were an infant's
　　smiling, sometimes weeping
he reworked into the teenager
　　I knew　　possessed　　loved:
still he chiseled towards a beauty
　　he paused to contemplate,
as if content: and resumes—
　　his sharp edges grave fan-like
traceries from her eyes. One day
　　he will chisel a fraction too far,
and there will be just that dust
　　to shake from his pants,
those chips to knock from his shoes.
　　But as she looks in the mirror,
shaking from his pounding, dabs
　　powder to soften his lines, I feel
tenderness　　rage　　helplessness
　　at how careless he is of the living
stone under his hand.
　　We surrender to his blows because
we must, whether or not he
　　dreams like us, somewhere, some-
time he will say *"Ah, that's it.*
　　You are the one. You can stay"
and stops.

FORSYTHIA

Every thing is echoed in everything. Death
    may walk supreme through that desolation

closest to nature's heart, the forest a city
    bombed to abandonment, the sky a blue sheen

    found on a sharp blade— yet from these ruins
emanates this heart-stopping light.
    Look where a bank of barren bushes rises

across the river: in spring their yellow brilliance
    blinds which even now I see in their bareness,

as though seeing one thing broken into pairs,
    life and death which, like love and hate,

    we know at heart are the same... Is death then
just the after-glow of that blooming never
    wholly done but always renewed,

that bareness transformed into living flame?
    I stare at these bleak limbs on fire

with the fire that does not consume
    but stuns the mind and humbles the heart

    and know nothing. The river flows, the bushes
are a clock ticking, full— bare— full— .
    I am bound to know each thing in sequence,

to bear equally that yellow echo and barren glow.

HERON

Old man heron stalks the bog channels
and pond, solitary, quawking when I
    startle him in this late, clement air—
spring's melt bared three brethren

    winter ice and snow overwhelmed,
and little clothes his hollow bones
    beyond the flesh of memory. Hawk and
kestrel coast the bog that forgets its

    cranberries and steps towards wildness,
young oaks and pines, tall grass and
    bayberry cover beds subtle fox and
coyote hunt, while wolf noses south

    as the forest retakes New England's
empty, stony farms. These hear   claw
    sniff   pounce through snow or pursue
countless voles, mice, rabbits, but when

    an arctic wind snaps off the last russet
and Indian red leaves— when sleet,
    not drizzle, snow not rain, drift and
patter from a pewter sky— old man heron

    skates across the pond, beak hammering
foot-thick ice until a night the stars scatter
    from their cold, icy heights and warmth
marbles outward in. He sees life's silver

flash in his black dream, draws back his
head to the painful edge of release—
    fox and coyote crouch in fear when
that great beak stabs upward into peace.

OLD FLAME

Long lingers the winter,
    longer each year—
spring pauses as though
    a bride in the aisle
changing her mind,
    summer takes so long
to shrug off her cold showers
    it flashes past a jet's trail,
soon dissolved in the sky:
    then fall burns a path
for winter, a tortoise
    in a frozen shell.
You and I smolder on,
    our children grown with
children, our passion that
    blinded whole afternoons,
bed creaking below our single
    body, sweat-slicked,
almost swooning when we
    wiped the taste of absence
from our blended mouths,
    worn down. Still
our coals heat the room
    however winter presses
at our door, each year
    that little longer,
each bridal spring that less sure,
    each summer shorter.
Cleave to me, love
    in our season of defiance:
we will set winter dancing
    in its shell, nonetheless.

AUTUMN LIGHT

The brilliance of this late light!
The sun at noon is low as late
    afternoon in summer, its light
honed to an edge summer forgets,
    sheathed in air crisp past the edge
of breaking. My fogged mind clears,
    heart soars, and I almost forget
this is not my spring, but autumn,
    that a leaner season has come
when apples left on the bough turn
    sweet and sag inward with frost's
first touch, when sap urges the root
    to prepare spring's burn through
winter's sleep. I envy wood's steadier
    strength— when my time comes
I will only sleep. Yet this light…
    To soar in the fall of an age, to find
life taste so sweet now gray sheathes
    my head! To feel my blood sing
instead of anger or despair clot its flow!
    Explain that. I will walk here as
sunset sharpens the air, never more
    alive than as darkness grows.

JESSE'S DREAM

Jesse windows were popular in the Middle Ages, showing a vine or tree or some leafy variation rising from Jesse's body revealing his descendants through the kings of Israel, starting with his son, David, up to Mary and Joseph, with Jesus at the top, crucified... This poem is based on the Jesse window of the Church of St. Mary the Virgin in Shrewsbury (England), which shows a tree of vines rising from a sleeping Jesse. The imagery springs from a passage in Isaiah about how "a rod (would grow) out of the stem of Jesse and a branch shall grow out of his roots: and the Spirit of the Lord shall rest upon him." The window was originally in nearby St. Chad's which collapsed in 1788, and was then moved to its present location.

1 Power

Arms encircle him, lips open
      tongue-hungry, as eager
         as she was shy
their wedding night:
      she pulls him into her,
         delights in his thrusts,
feels him soften, then stall
      "Jesse?"
         then recoil
from her womb
      that wants   wants
         and roll to his feet—
"Jesse, what's wrong?"
      He feels some power
         loose in the tent
still his words,
      buffet the walls,
         make the guy ropes snap

like a wolf who gnaws
    a trapped leg,
        better maimed but free:
feels that power use her
    to use him
        and stalks outside.
Power tugs at his robe,
    lifts dark dust-spirals
        around his feet,
becomes the wind that carries
    wolves' howls
        testing the night
for its promise. Impulse
    drives him through
        his restless flock,
fur ridged down the dog's necks:
    overhead stars reel
        as though he spins,
while the ground heaves
    underfoot: he drops down,
        clasps his knees, rocks
back and forth, afraid
    until he curls on his side,
        dazed.

2 His dream

His body is carried to a river's shore
    and grounds, slack-jawed, all still
until tendrils of roots shake loose
    from the earth and twine over sink
into him, curl   from his mouth:

then a blur of branches
flashes out from the tree
    that whirls upward
from his chest, his mouth
    an 'O' of terror:
bodies shape on it limbs,
    crowns on their brows
swords in their hands:
    he cannot speak, cannot
move   cannot wake.
    The crowns vanish,
manacles bind arms bind
    legs, a chorus of despair
lifts from contorted lips
    as the tree ascends
and, manacles gone,
    simpler men hold crooks
or carpenters' tools—
    No! he ties to scream
but power whirls that tree
    to where a man wavers
at its top thorn-crowned,
    arms akimbo,
a wound in his side,
    tossing words at the sky:

whirls his mind further
  where swords become guns
whose streams of bright
  bullets become rays
that make a lightshow of death.
  Then men in far rooms
rain down a pitiless death
  as they press buttons
before screens
  whose patterns shift...
Hovels fill the field,
  long halls colonnade
and rise on steel bones
  into bridged spires
filled with people
  who never cease to rush:
hearts in bright rooms
  throb in hands
that replace and heal
  until machines lie on
still breasts— they hum—
  the dead rise, take wing
in the snow in the heat
  of a burning winter,
the cold of a frozen summer.

His mind falls back
to the tree, he is the
    blood that runs from
the wounded man, molten
    he burns the faces, sears
branches, sets shepherd
    crooks ablaze, melts
manacles   swords   crowns
    scorches the trunk
flows down to his chest
    and runs into his veins—
he is red lightning-filled—
    "Noooo!"

In one startled motion he rolls
    to his knees, head down,
a dog panting, a man drooling,
    awake, heart racing: and fastens
his gaze on a pebble he grasps
    until hurt replaces everything.

3 Rebellion

Names race in his mind, David,
    his son
            "I have no son"
                        Solomon,
        Abias, Manasses, another Jacob,

Joseph, Jesus
          "I have no son,
  no crown, no chains— "
                    and again
    sees the man atop the tree

turn his face to the sky
  and speak, "forgive, forgive"
    "—no tortured death!"

I will let no murderous force
  move through me, a fire in the
    dry brush on our hills,

one spark and it burns for days
  until it finds water: none of that!
    he thinks. The howls grow,

soon the wolves will set on sheep:
  "Pass mine by, pass me..."
    But that upward whirl still

fills him with fear, the pain
  of that blood, his veins—
    then knows all at once

he is wrong, a child who grasps
  an elemental lesson, that the dream
    does not mean power released

but challenged, power
    made to face suffering,
        power dared to serve love.

4 Love

He forgets to breathe at that thought
    dangerous as Moses' burning bush
that leaves the bush unharmed but sears

the thrust-in hand— and remembers to breathe.
    "I am a simple man. A shepherd
with a new wife, who wants a son.

I ran into the night. I had a dream.
    That love might change, well, anything.
That such men, that such a man

could come from me." He smiles at how
    his wife's hunger drove him away;
what else should she feel?

Then feels such lust he staggers
    through his flock past the startled dogs
into his tent, walls sagging, wind still,

to where she waits.
                    "Jesse?"
                              Her mouth
    flowers under his, her breasts lift
full moons to his tongue, her belly

flows to his touch, a loose heap of grain:
    her thighs are water that trembles
over a slight fall as he enters her

unable to wait he fills her   still hard
    he moves in her laughter   in his
she is a harvest he cannot finish reaping

as he releases again and still stays hard:
    she pushes him away, washes him, his
hardness pulses in her hand

she falls back with a smothered laugh
    as he drives into her, again.
                   Pitiless the tree
whirls in his mind: its faces exult

and moan and cry as he flings love
    into the world's mix. Finally, so sweat-
slicked they cannot hold together

he falls from her into a well of sleep.

5 The wife

The woman always last, least, who is most, for whom we cease
    to be beasts in the field,
rests nameless on her elbow to brush the wet hair from his face.
She feels the night smile and wonders at the silence, if the wolves
    have fed and gone wherever wolves go:
if wolves make love.
They must, there are always more she thinks,
then wonders if Jesse will find less sheep in their flock.
Tonight, if ever, lamb and wolf should have lain together.
She knows he left because she was so eager, knows all they do
    must be his idea
and nuzzles his shoulder, for he will do her will if she waits.
"David:" she tries its sound: *we'll name our son David, by the time*
    he comes Jesse will be sure it is his idea.
Men make such trouble when the world moves in us to its ends, when
    we can only let it all come...
A howl blows downwind as she falls towards sleep imagining
    how she will rise again to his passion in the morning,
everything for him, whatever empires or churches rise and fall
    in his kiss:
how with each child the world is reborn:
how love dares everything, how everything is from love, how
    everything is, for love.

A WASP IN THE SUBWAY

homage to Camus

Have I dreamed of another life
   not shaken stop to stop
in brightly lit spaces between
   tunneled darknesses?
not strange among strangers
   but instead below a ball of fire,
unbound sky, buildings, yes,
   but gardens to strike prey
in the instant of desire:
   wind, clouds, rain, and nights
life-long compared to these
   flashing by? I have woken
to poverty, to myself, alone.
   That safety I once held,
a life known, is gone, and
   that sense of life eternal
in each moment, with so many
   to live! Now life feels too short
for memory. I smash against
   surfaces I cannot pierce,
against clarities that stop flight,
   tight-throated as a moth
must be who homes on fire,
   without answers. And then,
battered, at a pause, I am
   surprised by a wave of joy...
To lose all illusions, even hope,
   and have only my will
to go on: to make what I can
   of my flight despite

those crowded here, who raise
    their hands against all
they fear: what freedom! I race
    through their cringe and flail
free even of pity.

DANTE TO AN ADMIRER OBSESSED WITH LOVE AND FAME

Stop asking me about love: all I know
    is betrayal, injustice, rejection, dreaming:
my great love belonged to another
    and used her faithfulness to educate my lust.
Later I loved another too young for me:
    when I bared my feelings she spurned
my age, stonier than granite. Bitter poems
    helped; with the other I buried my sadness
in her perfection, my Beatrice, my paradise
    never mine, my emblem of God's grace.
For the rest? Moments of delusion in a world
    only those can love who lead lives
sheltered from the countless abuses we add to
    relentlessly. Don't think fame consoles
a love never gained, a love that then
    cannot be lost— I tell you, that love
is a chain wound tightly around the heart.

Once you asked what it meant when a woman
    returned your love and you dreamed
your dead mother watched you entwine. I said
    it symbolized constant love. I lied.
The truth is we die, and love with us.
    There it is, stonier than granite.
Do you grasp my real desire? To be loved
    for myself, to love my work, not use it for
my refuge; to have my heart's desire near
    while I can. Banal, dreaming, normal.

131

In the end, where can I rest? Not here
    where winds tear fine threads from
a cloud's edge in wintry Venice, and ice
    silvers the streets diamond-bright:
nor in Forli or Verona, Padua or Treviso,
    Lucca, Lunigiana, places I was driven to,
then fled: least in Florence that taught me
    exile follows exile— youth from childhood,
manhood from youth, home from homeland—
    until exile etched in the bone is my only home.

I will go to Ravenna to finish my poem,
    this comedy of life I cloak in the divine:
if I die there, lay me where emperors
    and empresses stare from the walls,
certain as angels by God, wherever He is,
    as Love, wherever She is: may they be
more than mosaics on a wall! Sometimes
    I dream my heart has no flaws
and the world no cruelty love cannot redeem,
    no stone it cannot touch to life and hope.
Then I waken here, or there, cut quills
    to a point, mix ink, smooth paper as dawn
spreads its spilled wine across the floor
    and steals another day from the night
in hope some presence will warm my words
    so the page before me has more on it
than breadcrumbs red stains and rage
    at this poor life I drink and you so admire.

Note: The poet's dream alluded to is drawn from one of the initial poems in Dante's *Rime*. The later, stony lover is drawn from the 'Pietra' poems towards the end of the *Rime*. Dante died in 1321 when 56 in Ravenna, for a time the late Roman and Byzantine capital of Italy and the West, after a lifetime of exiled wanderings through Italy. Ravenna is the home of famous mosaics of the Emperor Justinian beside his wife, Theodora. Dante completed the *Divine Comedy* there.

A HULA GIRL WEAVES DEATH AND MEMORY AND LIFE INTO HER DANCE

The sun has burned your taffeta bronze
    red flowers glow in your hair
bare-footed Tahitian hula girl
    native and new.
Your hands summon cloud shadows
    from the shore where they race,
and night, then day, alternate
    as your hips sway side to side:
you draw soft showers down
    the floodlights inflame, and dip
the Southern Cross with its white blaze
    into the nightblue sea.

Strange sails strange men stranger tongues
    come to a shore all green sparkle
at your nod: first English drums,
    then French whispers
full of sudden clarities and sibilance:
    each moves to your rhythm
with the gathering force of bullets
    that splash in bronze chests
in a futile fight for freedom.
    You comb your hair by the shore as
your love, bronze or a burned white,
    sleeps where a bed remembers
your shape: another sweep of your arms
    and stroke by stroke, gaze inward,
you brush an ever lighter blue
    into the sky—

and in one graceful gesture change
    the waves' surge over the reef
that creates the lagoon
    into your breasts' slow rise and fall:
music floats from you,
    from that source men hunger for,
violate, and hold in awe.

Your instep curls, and I remember
    your glow in my wife's cheeks,
new child in her arms after a night
    I gulped down Homer, waiting:
a smile, then as you look away
    I realize I saw your absence, too
in the white stone of my father's dead flesh,
    and heard you play the fifth
of Vivaldi's *Four Seasons*
    as my mother sighed a last time.
Worlds flash and fade with each turn
    each sway: now I smell you
in spring's violet evenings
    full of orange blossom and jasmine,
now in a reek I can nearly taste
    of flesh and acrid sand
where great machines seed death
    in violent, foreign lands.
You smile, your eyes meet mine,
    and I know I have felt you throb
in my 4 a.m. blood, then your fingers
    brush sleep across my brow, a presence
never there when I look, *yet there.*

Your hands still, the music stops: I and
    all enraptured know for one moment
that what is real is rare, that our lives are
    entangled, endlessly new and strange
you seed in an earth nothing exhausts,
    all pasts forgiven, and past recall,
demiurge, avatar, emblem of something
    we sense but cannot name.
The urge wells in me to dance in you
    all our days and nights, all
our heart's pain and all our heart's joy
    without end...

CROSSING ALBERT BRIDGE

No wind blows across the bridge
    as cars slide by on grease, fumes
motionless in the air. Light sheets
    the river so I can barely stare
past the Victorian froufrou of cables
    and girders to Battersea Park
and the building where William
    lives in his dream, an aging protégé
of Ezra Pound. A faint breeze stirs
    the light and fumes as I start to cross,
stronger with each step until
    it breaks the river's mirror into
sharp shards that water my eyes.
    He will offer tea, head bobbing,
eyes anywhere but on mine, a man
    far brighter than his mannerisms,
then talk of old poets young when
    he was; of his friend Peter, and
how Anita keeps him going,
    her light fingers tapping nearby.
He will clean after his crippled dog,
    stumble sorting his fax from
his telephone, praise my poems,
    someone new to leaven his familiars.
I smile and walk faster though the
    wind strengthens and clouds race
across a sky empty a moment ago.
    The air cools, cools more, the cars
wheel crisply, small waves rise
    to larger on the dull river where
a man in a skiff with a passenger
    struggles to make headway.

Halfway across the wind tears
    at my shirt and the papers I hold,
an anxious eye to the sky as gray
    locomotive streamers race under
rain clouds... Suddenly I'm sure
    he won't be there— I've mistaken
the hour, the day, the year—
    helmeted he is racing his motorbike
across a gray land— no, I remember—
    his drinking got out of hand,
his liver gave out, he was laid
    in a sterile room wife and child
silent at his side, the hour too late
    for forgiveness. He died. Nearly
across the wind's whoosh stops me
    as I lean forward though all
the park trees beyond are still,
    the buildings across empty
their windows blind eyes
    that take in and let out nothing.
One more step and I will be there
    determined to see another William
who directed my plays and
    'came out' at sixty and was happy
three years then his heart stopped:
    another step and I could find the
three hundred and eightieth floor
    my father assured me he was on
as angels circled my head: a last
    step and my mother's ashes will
move in reverse through the fire
    until she is in bed with Vivaldi
playing into his fifth season
    heard when she slid on one

easy breath into silence. I stare
  a moment more into that park
where no birds sing, sure
  my will can force my way—
and go back step by step the river
  stills though that oarsman goes on
to the farther shore. Cars slide by
  their fumes hang in the air as
the sky clears and the sun blinds
  the water: soon no breeze blows
and I'm off, Albert Bridge nothing
  I can't cross someday with a
wind at my back when I get the
  year the month the hour right.

WILD GIRL

White herons stand tall on tanned cliffs
    as a seal's splashes startle three otters from their sleep
        in the kelp:
there is no one else in this sheltered cove but a girl
    who gives me one glance only as I jump from the steep path
        onto the sand
that is enough to let me know I have invaded her privacy,
    and though no hounds stir at her call something deeper moves
        in her eyes
green as the sea's on a brilliant day as she sweeps back hair red
        as sea dulse—
                        call me crazy
    but I know she is the sea taken body to hunt her own edge
for the treasures she throws away in the sea-wrack,
    careless, profligate, a moment carefree in the light and air
from the pressures and currents within her depths....
    I look at the shells at my feet or rolling in the wavelets,
at the herons in silent prayer on the cliffs,
    the seal, the otters, the sky an altar of blue,
and only then realize she is gone.
    I never see her again. Even so
when the wind combs back a wave's crest like a girl's bound hair
    tossed loose
        I am certain the sea is alive and conscious,
a girl in this mood, a hag in savage anger with wild white hair
    in another,
        a woman still with grief who leans on a rock by calm waters
           on a gray day,

or one with child, her gaze inward as life stirs there.
   However the waves make my soul long for her infinite,
I know nothing will come to lessen that ache:
   the sea keeps secrets we barely guess—
we are meant to be limited.
   Yet when my eyes joined hers that day
I knew what she knows, that everything is ahead and always
   will be
      and for that moment was as young and ageless too.

ROOTS

This tree tilts westward where the sun
falls into the sea's renewing salt:
    half its roots writhe past the cliff into air,

half strain to hold crumbling ground.
    When the last grain of necessary earth
falls away this great tangle of experience

    sails into the air until it meets
the uprushing land. One wet season
    erases the cliff's wound and bares

the skeleton in the green cloud that fell.
    I swore then I would leave this place,
but instead a few roots test the air,

    while the rest grow knottier holding on.
If some part of me could find a home
    not marred by loss, I would speak a word

of timelessness, but the ground erodes
    underfoot, and now and then I wonder
how it feels to sail into a pure azure.

DANDELION

Ally of the massed flames of daffodils
    that scorch the air, invader of lawns
and verges of roads, you banish April's
    memory of winter with raw life.
Ragged-leaved, your tuberous stem
    roots in the ground's thaw to feed
the dayglo yellow of your angular sun
    more beautiful than the storied rose
or the honeyed argosy of Plato's words
    that bear his people down the ages:
than Lear demanding sense of the storm,
    or Einstein's vault of thought
where all changes to something strange.
    Yours is a light we can hold, a music
of the spheres we can walk on,
    your beauty greater than the peach's
furred recesses with their musky,
    womanly scent. When your sun dims
you become a white globe whose seeds
    my breath spin into the air
to float, fall, root, endure a long cold
    and against all odds quicken
when the earth turns towards the sun
    and once more looks to such as you
to lift death's hand from our throats.
    I wish you stood here, and I
flowered there.

WASTE FRUIT

A thin, sweet flesh embraces
the brown pits in these golden globes
    that hang among stiff, waxy leaves,
        but no one picks them from the
brittle limbs— they mottle, and drop
    rotting on the ground. Not squirrel
        nor night-eyed opossum care, nor
grosbeak or linnet, sparrow or
    doves, thrasher with his scream,
        thrush, or owl with stars for eyes...
All is wasted as those lives ruined
    by violence, or by living with one
        indifferent to what each has
uniquely to give, wasted as those
    with only themselves in their hearts,
        impenetrable, impoverished.
Tonight I wake from bad dreams
    as fear slips its leash to loom
        over my bed; breathless,
I hear the loquats whisper down
    the air to the ground's
        remorseless embrace. I dread
all I have to offer will be spurned
    as well, illusion be all I have
        to make life bearable to its end,
that the truth is hard and not my friend,
    our lives too often wounds to endure
        in silent despair as our ripeness
withers. At dawn light sculpts a dim
    guess of leaf and limb into the
        loquat tree that haunts my sleep—

but today I will shear off its fruit,
    stamp flesh and seed into the earth
       and hose the rest away
to lift its shadow from my heart.

BLUE WINGS

The sky spreads blue wings over the waking land—
where they will tire and fold only the stars know
who hold the mystery of their light in far, hot hearts.
Perhaps their feet are these branches whose green shoots
    spear past their buds;
perhaps they furrow these stubble fields.

Perhaps this blue is in my mind—
what February day could be so clear?
And it is gray, and cold, and a white rain sleets over
    a frozen earth.
Or are they just my all-too-human flight
from the burdens that wear us down—

from the bitterness of a child who disappoints,
or our impotence when we cannot help;
from a life fallen short of our dreams
we bury in praises of 'the real',
or from the endless varieties of abuse

we heap on each other with malice or willful self-deceit?
Nonetheless
I will walk under their all-embracing flight as they beat
    unbarred by any cloud
borne on the earth's brown river past all
that cruelty and death thought they could freeze, forever.

GREAT UNHAPPINESS GREAT JOY

Coyote cries carry down a wind
    that adds a wolf howl from the eaves:
night falls on woods late heat burned
    then storm stripped, so autumn is
betrayed into winter before winter.

Against the long, Atlantic dunes
    waves stutter with mounting anger
while wet snow piles heavily inland
    and breaks leaf and wire then boughs
to sheet the roads with debris,

a night Lear tears at the sea-walls
    or ranges the moors and woods
that shake with his rage and fear
    his bare hands, spume-soaked beard,
his howls the wind's...

Would there was a blank place on a map
    labeled 'World's End', a place known
only by warm rivers that flow from a
    heartland where we imagine
no tremble in the light reminds us

of wings and a sword brandished
    to bar return, where neither
the world nor innocence is marred.
    Instead as this heavy-handed
nor'easter thumps to come in

we savor cranberry muffins
  fresh-buttered from the oven
that melt on our tongues—
  and debate what latest cruelty
we have done each other

to plumb again the well of forgiveness
  that lets our lives go on, common,
human, at times humane,
  without recourse to the greatness
only great unhappiness calls forth.

On the morrow as the storm recedes
  we survey its ruin, near blind
from the clear light, and think soon
  amid holiday cheer we will mark
birth in the death of the year,

while at twilight when leaf and limb
  release some of the light they took in
so each glows in its own hue,
  just then, for one moment, despite all,
we too feel lit from within.

WESTON WOODS

How green the dark in Weston woods—
    if you look for me here in after years
I will not be haunted, or haunting,
    but imbued in a seam of bark or a rustle
of leaves or the heft of a stone from a long,
      low wall—
    and if you sense my stare, turn quickly—
we will be face to face. In these woods
    the years are leaves that never fall
but flutter around me so time so irreversibly
      one plus one
    runs every way down these paths, splits,
      circles,
          rejoins,
all entangled:
               the car I gun up an icy hill
    into a tree;
    a woman a girl mine who melts beneath me
as the Sound licks the shore and sighs roll
      off the swells;
my father who slaps me after a graduation
      all-nighter;
my daughter who steps on a copperhead
    too lazy to turn and bite— she is three,
      and death sleeps:
and me, who time out of mind strains for
    sense in these woods.
Fireflies begin to light the dusk. Here
    they are on and off at once, like ourselves,
      at once dark
        and blazing.

CAPE COD WOODS

Autumn and winter storms spin down
   from the north and work spumes
      of salt sea spray
into the rich moraine that shaped this arm
   bent into the sea
      and stunt the pines: peace
does not settle here as in inland woods
   even when the maples and oaks are
      heavy with green as a woman with child—
instead their hush holds the before and after
   of storm, a peace treasured more for
      being hardwon and transient.
Once I found gravestones in the woods,
   names erased but upright, the sense of
      human passion and blood spilled
in the past part of the brightness,
   and felt myself more at home
      in that taut balance between extremes
than in the tall soliloquies redwoods speak
   to time near my Pacific home, or in
      the countless years that garden English
woods and fields into a child's fantasy.

One day the bearlike Atlantic
   will claw to its breast all but a few green-
      skirted hills, the air heavier still
with salt, even the maples and oaks
   forced to grow low as these pines—
      even so, my spirit is easy here,
at one with some calm-seeming afternoon
   after the stringent lash of some nor'easter,
      at home in the green saline tang, the
salted loam, the troubled peace.

THE CYPRESSES OF ATHENS

Tourists haunt placarded groves as though
   immortals puzzled equally by loss
and what endures in this ruin-rich ground.

   Longer acquaintance might let me name
these sparse, rain-starved trees:
   there *Agave*, blinded by a god,

who tore her son apart with her revelers
   when he spied on them, unable to believe
reason could not conquer passion:

   there *Plato*, followed by students
who fail to see how all these are copies
   of one perfect Cypress no one can find

that yet embodies seedbud to mature tip,
   withered tree to one wrapped in the green
flag of its foliage:

   there *Oedipus*, who died holy though
his children were his sisters and brothers,
   buried nearby under streets where taxis

cheat the unwary,
   his crimes all efforts to avoid his fate,
that force we make come true.

   That cypress whose green is nearly black
is a priest who beheaded old gods:
   that a Turk who holds his robes against the wind,

while next to him Byron
  who died, despite his irony, for Greece
twists upwards below this severe light.

  One day a descendant of mine wandering here
may name some cypress in turn:
  'Ah! there's *Lance*! He always wanted

to balance passion with reason,
  desire with desire's loss,
his life with his death in a tense balance

  like one of these cypresses
who thrust out green shoots against their withering,
  defiant to the end'.

I wander in their shade as the light pours down;
  its brilliant rain ignites a newer jet of green
to replace each that fails and falls

  to this parched, incendiary ground.

MY FATHER'S SHADE AT DELPHI AT THE WORLD'S CENTER AMID THE RUINS ABOVE THE OLIVE-SWADDLED VALLEYS

I cannot bear so much loss.
    A few stones, fewer columns,
some tiers of seats, a ruined
    arena, a thousand years of faith
gone with the temple where
    they carved, "Know Thyself"
over the entrance. That command
    still lives in my blood.
I remember the old ritual
    and let some fall from a cut
for any shade to drink
    and take body from for
an hour, but it is my father
    who surprises me here.
"Why have you neglected me?"
    he demands. "Why are you
so far from Los Angeles
    where your ashes lie?"
"All places are the same in death."
    "I loved you," I answer,
so many years of anger
    spent to let me say that:
"but you hurt us all so pointlessly
    and shrugged your guilt away."
He goes away angrily as
    the hot air warms these stones...
Below, groves of olives
    paint the valleys graygreen.

ΓΝΩΘΙ
ΣΕΑΥΤΟΝ

Art by Ron Sanford

Their fruit is too bitter to eat
    unless soaked and steeped
until like the hardest memory
    we forget their native state,
and eat. I douse my head under
    what's left of the muses' spring
and shake the droplets off
    like a dog when I stand.
What is the world?
    that this place, once its center
was so forgotten we had to
    dig it out
to find what we charge
    tourists to contemplate?
What is time?
    Just now, the water still cold
on my face as I take in the heights,
    the olive-painted valleys,
I know: *time is nothing*.
    My father, nothing
but what I make of him, then
    and now. Myself, nothing
but what I make, then and now.
    I don't need a sibyl's fumes
to give me a madness
    for others to mine for sense:
the world is empty of everything
    but this constant remaking.
Know thyself.
    It is almost more than I can bear.

Delphi, 2013

ABSENCE IN ITHAKA

If this island belonged to me, I would bury
    all my books and never go away.... Byron

There are more tourists than rain
    on the more famous islands,
        for the centuries sleep in Ithaka
with no trace of its famous past.
    Profuse clusters of grapes hang over
        the balcony above the closed
Communist Party Office
    a block from the harbor
        which the town bends its U around,
the houses that climb the hills flashing
    in this light,
        that light in this water through this air

sharp and clear as an edge of broken glass.
    I feel as odd in this waterside taverna
        as I did my first night in London
when I walked into Sloane Square's
    King's Head to the tune of *Hotel California*,
        a Los Angeles boy whose home follows
him everywhere.
    Ithaka could be Catalina
        with the same chaparral-clad hills,
the same light half a world away,
    my head full of stories, like Odysseus',
        always tempted to think at each landfall

'I could forget everything here and be
    something new',
        yet who stayed himself everywhere
until after twenty years
    of wading through blood
        he stood again beside his Penelope
and only then remembered
    he never wanted to go.
        What holds one forgetting to another,
one story to the next, one strange life
    to another,
        each departure to a return

through and above or below
    all the upheavals that make their ways
        into our histories, stories, dreams?
As I puzzle
    a young couple stroll along the harbor
        hand-in-hand
fresh from love made
    in a cool room before the sun
        could turn their caresses to sweat-soaked
gropings and groans.
    Did they walk this way after Odysseus left,
        when the Romans came, and Byzantines,

Venetians and Turks, and again the Greeks?
   Because their serene walk beside the water
      in whose sparkle Aphrodite still dances
gives all those histories, stories dreams
   their ground:
      love anonymous except to lovers,
not when swept away
   but in those moments when they know
      they will share themselves again
to heal the heart's harms, and complete
   the world— love standing
      however absence piles an absence
against the tides of oblivion.

TIDE & TIME ON CAPE COD

This brilliant spring light
   is a drug I come down from
      in shades of gray
that deepen into night:
towards dawn rain falls,
   the dwarf pines and oaks'
      early leaves
stream in the wind.
                Later,
the front blown out to sea,
   the light again makes
      my blood leap,
but not my friend's—
the chambers of her heart
   keep separate beats
      unless medicated.

Is she consoled as catkins burst
and crows harry a hawk
   whose red tail flashes
      as he banks away?
as yellow warblers twitter
in the vines and redcapped
   woodpeckers taptaptap
      the pines,
while a cardinal weaves
red ribbons through the trees?
   All here is change—
      a winter ago, or two,

a wild sea thrust
through the spit of sand
    speared south from Nauset
        to island its tip
that even now migrates
south to Monomoy—
    waves swept away
        homes once safe
on Chatham's shore:
the Cape entire will slide
    under the rising wave,
        replaced by remnant
isles and islets— sails
will skim new channels
    and ferries pick their way
        as much by guesswork
as not as the sea wears
what's left of the old moraine
    into the depths,
        grain by grain.

Roll, Atlantic stormswells,
pierce the land, carve
    new futures from the
        swept-away,
unready, over-confident,
unthinking, those in denial,
    those aware, and those
        just biding their time.
Along the new shore
driftwood will drink in
    the light as dry earth,
        rain,

or dull in fog or storm,
laid where the tides will
   until taken for fire.
     There it will be
transformed into lucent
blues, reds that echo
   sunset or dawn,
      greens
like the sea's, the steel
blue becomes in the cold,
   the sun's noon yellow.
     Inland, roots will delve
deeper in the lost graveyard
I found on a piney knoll,
   islanded in
     that future sea,
holding children who once
ran and laughed, and mothers
   who sighed
     with impatience
calling them in, all
changed to rich soil
   and a tang of salt
     on the breeze,
their spirits now stormwind
that uproots with abandon,
   now the deep silence
     of still woods—
or the pent moment of slackwater
where ebb and flow are
   held in balance—
     as once was every star,

every laugh, or sob or
lover's cry, every crime
   every poem or forgetting
     and every heart
that will ever confuse its rhythms
once held in a point
   too small to measure,
     a silence too deep
to plumb, a balance so filled
with extremes
             its burst
   still runs up that shore
     we call time
with no sign of sinking
into the sand before
   a following wave.

   Now fog dulls the light
on this cool, April day:
blackheaded terns hunt
   the Sound's restless edge,
     hover, then dive:
wings flash, they lift from the
waves and pass overhead
   as others take
     their place, a scene
so common I imagine
no matter how far I go
   from this salted,
     wave-splashed, windy,
shell-and-seaweed-littered shore
this scene is always there.
   I fill with anger
     because it is not so—

and with a sense of marvel, too,
because as I stand here
    I am already changing
        into something new
and strange.

ON THE BEACH

Westhampton, 1950 -1958

The girl I love each summer
   is beside me on the beach
so close I smell her skin
   with its wash of freckles
across her cheeks and nose.
   We never say 'I love you',
everything about us is too fresh.
   A light breeze ripples the
summer Atlantic, puffs a few
   grains of sand in the air
as I soak in the sun, the heat,
   her smell, my salted flesh aglow.
The sea-grass sparkles green,
   the scent of sand mingles
with salt as soft waves roll in,
   the memory of winter gone
as if winter itself is gone,
   when winter is coming.
I feel complete: what do we
   have to do with time and tide?
We are in flood, and ebb
   seems outside belief— except
as the constant self sees
   one image follow another
in the mirror as though in a
   slide show, as I do daily now,
thinking these cannot all be me,
   then that 'I am' is an illusion,
but not unreal, for these
   dreams are my realities.

One spring day after we
    have been apart all winter
her laughs go up in the air,
    startled birds: she is ironing
and speaks of a boyfriend
    who will be here soon—
and I understand, so heavy-
    hearted, so innocent, he
will walk beside her on the beach.
    Older, we live more distant,
unguessed others tug us away,
    coming here is harder—
already our past becomes
    images of summer idylls
swept free of shadows
    where I am uniquely happy
and she less herself than
    those idylls' symbol
magnet, earth, although
    it was the beach, the crab
and clam rich bay, the sea,
    the stars I lay beneath alone,
the ocean's counsel in a
    treasured solitude
that drew me and
    consoled all troubles.
The flutter of those wings
    deafens... I step outside
for the first time old enough
    to feel how our lives are
passages and forsakings.
    We never meet again.
But even now there are times
    when we walk hand in hand

down the shore, inchoate
    with longing, stealing looks
at each other, everything flesh and
    fresh as the beach stretching
ahead of us without end.

A NIGHT IN THE MOUNTAINS AFTER A DOWNPOUR UNDER STARLIGHT

1.

And do the mountains still stand, arms hanging, giants
    who ponder the stars?
or have they folded into the green clouds of the canyon's walls,
    sheathed in sycamore and oak and red-limbed madrone
to sleep away the day?

And does the light dance on monkey flower and indian
    paint-brush, red petals flickers of flame,
and on mountain lilac, blue and white,
    and on all the green leaves and red where poison oak
confuses the season?

How pungent their smell to obliterate the salt tang of the
    sea breeze...

And is this my arm that aches, my hand grown so heavy, my
    breath so short?
when once I climbed to this waterfall with a light step, paused,
    and pushed higher into the mountain?
Now I let downpour's waters that flood down a chute and

arch over a lip of rock into the over-flowing pool at its foot
    drown my breathing,
thoughts of how, lower, bridges were swept away so I
    forded back and forth on the trail until it rose
distract me as pain subsides in my arm.

I decide to stay the night, and work my way downcanyon
    to a quiet pool where
the sky tunnels between the leaves, and settle...
    Blue deepens to twilight, purples,
and at some point I cannot describe goes starfield on field...

They will wonder where I am, a woman pace, a child ask
    for me, a daughter reassure
He can take care of himself
    against the woman's
He should have called

2.

The giants shed their green cloaks and rise against the night
    to resume their questioning—
If anything lasts, even the stars, that are not the same
    as those in our youth?
If there is a god?

If even a mountain's life is a flash of light on water to him?
    If all is no more than a kaleidoscope in constant motion to his eye?
If there is neither life nor death then but only constant novelty?
    The water's liquid syllables answer, the leaves' rustle,
a scatter of stones as a hoof slips and a black muzzle dips
    to drink;

a silence   defined by our absence, a language my heart
    grasps but cannot speak—
and a phantom presence, barely sensed, that moves in
    the waters   leaves   sky   dipped muzzle   lift
    and fall of the mountains,
a power with no need to act, that acts: a   question...

3.

The mountains kneel as the light pearls, pinks, then turns
      day-hued: homeward I find the stream sunken into
      the ground
but for a pool here, a trickle there, its sluice-roar stilled, new
      bridges in place:
                              have I dreamed?
Has heavy-handed death on his stone throne stolen a season
      from my life?

Home they are urgent in demands, reproaches, for
      reassurance— how can I tell them the mountains
      debated time   purpose   fate?
and folded into the canyon's walls as I stood with a groan
      to start home?
She is there, her careworn face I see through to the untouched

sixteen year old I knew, and all the faces between:
      and her love that loves me   and makes my hand feel light.
Her dare to care awes me, so human-fragile, so powerful,
      despite all change the cause that makes the causeless
move, and search, and hunger   and delight.

ARS POETICA

Anxiety burns my stomach as I pace my night woods
    consumed with shadows of dry, machined, convenient,
      dead and repeated things.

Quick, heraldic beasts tease my mind as I search
    for firmer ground
      before I recall the smells of wet cypress,

floor-foresting pine needles and cones, and the whiff
    of kelp torn free by waves maddened by storms from
      Mexico, and piled along the high tide line

where flies mat the sand.
    These bring me to myself,
      and the coal of this woman in plowed sheets

whose nipples in the night are dark as blue juniper berries,
    whom I fan and furrow and seed.
      I remember what it means to be a man,

to give love, and receive, to hold those loved firmly,
    to protect, to respect, to live, to die
      on earth, in earth, of earth.

My hackles rise, and the short hairs on my arms
    as words flow that give each their true name,
      as the poem wells from my throat

        speaking me.

SELECTED
SEQUENCES

DANTE IN LOS ANGELES

four imitations after Dante

Selected artwork by Michael Foreman

These are very free versions of poems found in Dante's collected lyrics, the *Rime*. The first three are drawn from the Pietra series of impassioned but flinty love poems Dante wrote to a young, unresponsive woman in his maturity. The woman is never named beyond being called a stone in one way or another, and is unknown. The impact of her refusal provoked a psychologically realistic response in Dante new in a medieval poet and unlikely to be expressed absent real experience. "Exile" is based on "Amor, da che convien", the last of the poems gathered in the *Rime*. It is not one of the Pietra poems, and not addressed to the same young, rejecting woman. I would like to think these versions give a taste of the poems as they might have been had Dante written them now, in Los Angeles.

I MARBLE

after Dante's "Io son venuto"

When December strings Orion
in the canyons' throats, and touches
their summits with rare snow, Saturn
glitters like sunlit ice and Venus
vanishes in daylight. Then I might tell stories
of a doomed hunter, a god of a golden age,
or a goddess surfing on dawn's foam,
but in Hubble's universe tireless stars race
from each other through endless winter,
and skies full of metal spies hold no epics
or romances. So I chase without pause
in this woman's wake who is colder
than an airless rock in space.

More often we burn in false summers
when winter winds press through our
canyons from the desert; or Mexican
rains drift north and drench us warmly
until a storm from Alaska rolls
down the green wave of the coast
to clear the air with almost frozen rain
and dress our mountains in white.
Such tumults should distract me from
my private Monroe or Harlow or Stone,
but hot cold wet arid, these polar reversals
echo my own moods as I pursue this woman
who doesn't care if I am false or true.

Now cedar waxwings, starlings and
swallows have flown, and fluttering,
gaudily orange monarchs. Cats
that howl and mate all summer
silently stalk abandoned yards:
bulls in our mountain ranches
dream below sycamore and alder. I envy
their great mass of muscle, dull mind,
treetrunk limbs— no girl-cum-woman
weighs them down with constant denials.
Age grows heavy on my shoulders
as in greener times those bulls
on cows they mount, bellowing.

Yet narcissus blooms by Christmas,
then violets stain the garden blue:
acanthus leaves I cut to the ground
grow large as elephant ears... By February
white flowers dot the plum's bare limbs,
and tulips part resisting earth as they
spear upward from their bulbs—
sex is always rampant, here... Look at me,
lusting for this young thing though
she shoves me aside the way
soft shoots crack and move concrete.
This must be hell, I think, in constant fear
some other will see her bud and open.

Dante in L.A.

Too much or too little tells our story—
the creeks run dry, or rampage
as hills too full of rain fall to the flood
bubbling over rock and log as though gas
exploding from some deep earthquake-
opened rift: bridges and homes, dams,
and plows meant to shore hasty levees
are all swept out to sea. And when, later,
the scum of standing pools turns green
as corroded copper, I am no better off,
but still chase her with a lethal happiness,
starting to love what I hate— shame, and
suicidal thoughts my helplessness awakes.

What will happen if she stays as hard
when mockingbirds come home and sing
every love song they know all night long,
dancing in the trees' dark leaves?
I'll hold her in my heart anyway, and turn
by inches into what I want, as all men do,
even if that means growing marble-hearted, too.

II SEA STONE

after Dante's "Al poco giorno"

This woman is a stone, a whitening of grass,
a day circling into shadow, a cold that burns:

even so
my hunger stays green in her white hills

whose hardness belies her beauty.
When the year turns and hills burn green and
    flower,

I cling to her heels like a shadow
though she stays cold as snow in shade:

when she garlands her hair with laurel and ivy,
I am bound to her hard flesh more than a stone set
    in cement—

and when she dresses in green, so lovely, so lying,
I crawl after her, chewing the grass she walks on

though I am touched by gray and know better.
She turns the shade of trees to asphalt that burns and
    cracks from cold,

the grave to remembered misery without release—
even dust forgets its hunger for life in her shadow.

I would eat through her dry hills if a river,
wear shale into sand, make her flower:

or slice her foot if a sharp flint hidden in grass
mingling blood with garlands torn from her hair
    in pain.

That might not change her nature, but I would be
    glad,
for she is a stone made in darkness and cold and
    crushing weight

I cannot take from my heart
however she weighs me down and makes me old.

III SCENES FROM A MOVIE

after Dante's "Cosi nel mio"

Pursuit

Others envy me on the street
with this young woman on my arm,
but she goes no farther, thwarting
my experience and desire.
I crave her as a man does
afraid his passion is his last,
shamefully stringing myself along
although I should forget her.
She seems slight, but every word
tells me this woman is a killer
who never needs to say *No*
but lets me stay because she knows
I know how little she cares.

Montage

My mind flowers on the stalk
she holds in marble hands.
Or I am the ocean's flat plate
she crosses bored, untossed.
She is a rasp, and my soul
the wood or steel she grates:
or she gnaws on my heart
as though on the treat
a rat threads its maze towards.

Every woman I have loved
and let go adds to her power,
especially those who were better:
Not this time, I swear, and am lost.

Exposed

Alone, anguish is the monkey
driving me down the street
where I shout her name
like a homeless person delusion-
hagged, oblivious, only afraid
she will see me and laugh.
Here's a duel well past obsession!
I thought those stories romances
that make love a primal power
stronger than mind and will—
but look at me now, a man
who goes on loving a woman
who chooses to be cruel.

Committed *

Again and again I raise my hand
against myself— this straitjacket
pins my arms— the movement
is in my mind: I am not well.
I butt against a padded wall,
cry, no yell, until hoarse, still
not believing I'm here as blood
rushes to my heart and leaves me
white, swollen, enraged, faint.

184

I split apart and hit myself so hard
another blow from this familiar
stranger will kill. Yes, yes I know
this is just ingrown, rejected passion—

**

if only I could let loose on her!
But she breaks me apart
in daylight or shade, at dawn
or twilight, assassin, robber, this
dove hard as a diamond!
I'm in a hot, close place and howl,
hungry to hear her yowl, too—
and if she did, would forgive her
all. Then I would play with
her blonde hair and whisper
I'll help you, knowing
surprised by such kindness
she might start to love.

Dream

Her hair whips my face, my chest...
I grab and urge her on all
one afternoon and evening
with bearish caresses, consumed
with revenge but never hurting.
I just tease, sure, full of menace,
staring into those jasper eyes
that make my blood hot as lava
pouring through green shade.

She may be slow to kindle,
but once the damage she's done
burns her to a guilty response,
we live through tumults of peace.

Release

Woman, I give you up but don't
let go, waiting to see you treated
the same. Revenge? I am the image
of your neglect and live in winter,
old and small and bitter.

IV EXILE

after Dante's "Amor, da che convien"

What brute, possessive power
   drives me after this woman
      beautiful as rainfall sparkling
from a bright, clear sky?
   Who cold-shoulders love aside
      no matter what I do
or how my failures
   estrange me from my self?
      She floats overhead at night
and robs me of sleep:
   it's shameful
      how my body hardens and
my breath grows short
   as though she is there—
      no wonder I shout

in the house, on the street,
   ready to pin back anyone's ears
      who will listen,
a middle-aged man who jumps
   through any hoop malice
      puts in her hands.
I'm crying, see,
   but not from grief—
      opening her locked door
would make me whole,
   but passion rides me
      like a tree the wind

blows hard enough to break:
   as dead wood snaps off, the new
      takes the wind's shape.

Friends, I'm in trouble:
   her image is so alive
      in my mind, it drives
after the woman it's modeled on:
   I follow like a prisoner
      crazy enough to run
towards execution,
   futile as snow
      falling on the sun.
She is there too,
   and watches unmoved
      as a uniformed thug
makes me kneel and
   bends my head
      and cocks his gun...

So I learn to walk dead
   in sense, spirit or soul,
      morally dead, not mad,
driven to learn how
   a man goes outwardly on
      while ridden by a force
our words and tepid lives
   we think we regret
      have lost expression for.

Animal and cunning,
   I would wallow in coarse
      frank sex to win her,
or be pure as black light
   however she strips me to my
      subhuman raw.

Even this river that flows
   past the childhood home
      I left, never dreaming,
uprooted, I would be
   a stranger everywhere,
      leaves me inconsolable.
Along the banks, raspberries
   open white flowers,
      and barely unfurled leaves
mottle the bare limbs' brown
   while she holds me encased
      in polar ice...
And if I could come home,
   be at peace, and always warm,
      I know what I would say:

my heart is sore from her denials;
   let no man say he aches more:
      yet I will stay if she relents,
unrepentant by her side
   a stranger to everything but
      my own exiling love.

LATE SPRING

poems on the passing of my father

What A Man Gives
My Father's Song
Father Death
Haunting
By Love's Doing
Virgin Spring
Late Spring
Soft Weathers
Peace

WHAT A MAN GIVES

I

A heart exploring its inward flaw,
a bone its wither, a leaf quivering
on the branch, a breath of air...

He frightened my youth,
a domineering, hostile man:
now I wonder if he will fall
as once he fainted into my arms
paying for lunch at Nate & Al's:

bills flapped in the air,
coins wheeled across the floor,

but he recovered and hurried off,
a street actor improvising for a later show
while the ambulance I called
ferried up Beverly Drive all siren,
turning each gray head...

II

Sometimes he is a house
whose rooms are grieving old women
who draw black shawls tight,
for my sister and I rarely visit here—

some love-starved child in him
made him starve those he loved in turn:
now he goes room to room,
an old child wondering where
his sundered family has gone.

He was the son less loved
by a woman so foolish
she chose between twins: early and late,
their photos show him glowering
while his twin smiles smiles

                     smiles.

So he is doomed to be compressed
by love until he goes, for he fears
the more deeply love is held
the more certain love must fail.

III

Mother tired of the women
he denied to her but regaled
to me. He split himself in two
in three, in… and thought
he was faithful to mother's part.

Now at lunch young waitresses
dote on him, smiling
at his flattery; they see
the shadow of a ladies man,
while he swears me to lie

so his second wife, younger
than his daughter, won't know
we dine in regal elegance,
lamenting "The folly of
this marriage I endure

for fear the stress of breaking
it will break me too.
I've had bad luck in women,
I've loved unwisely. I suffer
from chronic heart chronic

skin disease— some days
I'm so tired it hurts to stand.
My career gives no solace,
devoted to ephemera:
the years are stones that grow

and bear me under."

IV

When unleavened darkness rises
will he hear a song
that braids all half-measures,
failures and shames
into a larger harmony?
Or dream some wild gesture,

skydiving with no parachute
to grasp death in pure defiance
expansive, released,
for choosing makes free
whatever its end?

At last put to rest
the need to be first
that gene and early accident
conspired role by role
to make him miss,

and now give all he could
or would or should? No,
who does? He will whisper, if he can,
once there is no other choice,
or signal a final 'yes' to pull the plug,
and sink, emblematic to the end.

V

I will mourn him long and hard
and hold my sheaf of sung defiances
to slow the fading of anger and love—
only accidents of time bring

virtues to light, and not faults
to condemn a man past recall:
only pride makes a man deny
all men are of a kind.

My heart explores its inward flow,
my bone its wither— I am a leaf quivering
on the branch, a mere breath of air...

MY FATHER'S SONG

My blood is singing
behind my right eye.
I am half blind with song.
From the left
the world lurches,
me side to side.
Pains hound
across my chest after
what fox, what hare:
I feel their fear.
My right leg
declares its presence,
my right forearm aches
as though raked and torn—
suddenly I know
I am the goal
of the fleet savage feet.
Is this a stroke descending?
Or am I feeling
the mortal state
my father feels
in his barren room,
ticking after the seconds
his eyes chase
around the clock?
We are less separate,
less I/Thou than we think.
My blood is singing
his song, and his? Note

by note he scales
towards that silence
I fear one day will be
all of song I hear.

FATHER DEATH

Twice I had to say "Yes, that's him"
first when my father died at the home
open-mouthed between breaths,
second at Mt. Sinai where a dwarf
wheeled him in silent and bloodless
as if stunned from seeing God.
I lied identifying him— we are the
    flesh's fire
not that residue there, not slag!
The dwarf leaked coldness, his face
    fine featured
but squashed, and pure white:
I had stumbled into nightmare.
How had he closed my father's mouth
that no one not me could do at the home?
Are the dead blocks of ice we hammer
    we chisel?

I'm watching a pretty girl as I write.
I imagine her breasts in my mouth
her milk, the rich cream of life: I need
an image to banish my father's
that rolls into view with his dwarf
when I make love, when I sit in the sun
when I examine my guilts, when I
recall our long rivalry, all unneeded.
I should have lied the truth, "No,
    that's not him":
what would they have done? Rolled in
    a series of stiffs?
'No, not him.   Not him, no.   Sorry, no'
but as usual I conformed. "Yes," I said,

and the hearse took him off; "Yes,"
and the dwarf wheeled him out.

Later when I walk by the ocean beneath
    the Milky Way
as I have done since I was ten
to find silence and self to frame
the tensions we call living,
I fit words to the surf's rhythms like
"Live, there is only living, each star
lives in its own milky fire; the hottest
blood burns in the coldest water:
why, father death lives in our flesh
to free us from anxious self-knowledge
when that burden grows too great"—
but I know these only gloss the unpleasant
    truth:
he must fade the way he died, by inches...

There should be more to us when we live.
There should be more to us when we die
than a bleaching like a photo left in the sun—
we aren't mayflies for a season,
not one of the countless ants:
but he after one "I don't know if I can do this"
faded steadily into distance,   aware   helpless
    acquiescent.
                    Better to go mad.
Only now, after so many years listening
do I know what the waves really say
as they beat against my anger:
forgive   forget   forgive   forget   forgive

HAUNTING

A wind wheels over the meadow
and breaths through my mind
as I relax by an empty house.
Clear across the bog I see the fox's corner
where the dogs always slaver against
their chokechains. Then, inside, I hear
a faucet turn, water run, stop, a footstep fall.
I *know* it's my friend's dead daughter, Canda,
wandering where she once lived.
I freeze, changed utterly in a second, afraid
of whatever comes through
when the wall between worlds, tumbles.
The next moment I *know* it's not her
but my father touching unfamiliar things,
a door   a faucet   a drawer
treading a strange hallway, his breath
making a daddy longlegs tremble,
determined to find me and never let go.
I'm terrified. My friend calls, *Lance*—
I breath, myself again, but what is that—
how easily I walk with the dead,
whether ghostly or just some bodying
of guilt and loss! I worry at that
like a dog at a fox's scent: I imagine
I slip my chokechain and dash
into those shadows folded into the light,
teeth bared, snarling, sure of my prey—
and find myself stumbling among presences
just this side of known... At a loss,
I turn a faucet: water runs through my flesh
like blood. I tread a strange hallway,
make the spider tremble in turn,

touch an arm— *Please, I'm lost, don't run,*
don't freeze so in terror at my face—
I only want to go home— .
I snap to. Now I know what sound
teases just beyond the edge of hearing:
it is the sound walls make when they crumble—
and walls are always falling down.

BY LOVE'S DOING

Blind in this darkness
I edge over the smallest rise, afraid
    to fall,
the ocean's weight on my shoulders;
or recoil from accordioned wrecks
as I follow the dream thread to caverns
that open and shut like mouths.

I stop:
my father's body whitens that dark
where death is the only light—
or a window full of sky where I press my
    three year old face
shines before me, full of inexpressible longing
for a father always walking away.

So I imagine
when the woman beside me flutters the sheets,
    hot-limbed, restless,
so long unable to wake me as I dreamed.
I am painfully sad, and think
I whitened those depths, but slid away
when I tried to touch my own death.

I'm not sure what images are true:
we always try to give face to the inexpressible,
or discover one story disguises another,
even feel sorrow we only fear may come—
    like I may rehearse in a past loss
the death I will owe at the end.

Only the pain is sure, and entire.

I reach for the woman, desperate
to be pulled into flesh, love, life
   by love's doing,
                        away
from that marrowed pain, from my childish face
pressed full of longing to the window;
   from knowing now love will leave
whatever I do to make it stay.

VIRGIN SPRING

Is my rage done, plowed into the meadow,
grief let loose in the rain, the desperate drive
    to change everything
burned out by distance and sun, as much to say
time is space   heat   loam   leaf in the air?
How quickly loss doesn't matter, not really, not
after the first boil of blood, whatever trace
    stays in memory:
for what grief goes on intense now as then—
some too intense knowledge there is no
but there for the grace of God go I
    when all go that way;
some unbalanced likening of self to self lost
so we go on grieving after father death
mother death   child death   for ourselves?
For me life breaks in, fog, rain, sun, the stars
    on clear, crisp nights,
wind, love, those still here or newly come.
We are the blood pumped through the great
    heart of things,
driven in spent and expelled readied
    for new losses—
like leaves that pile on the ground, decay,
    sink down, become rare
lady slippers in the woods or shoots
that crack concrete, delicate yet steady as steel.
Nothing is still, nothing stops.
Even the words that died into my loss
I could not imagine returning, return
when all seemed used, misused, and done,
gushing from my ground in a virgin spring.

LATE SPRING

Where has it hidden, this late spring?
Only now pheasants call like rusty gates
    forced open,
the air at last so warm and clear
Great Point Light is visible over twenty miles
    of Sound.
Heat ribbons the pines' resin through the trees,
and robins, in a fur of feathers in flight
seize the moment to mate and mate and mate.

And I— two years tending my father's dying—
peer into the marsh where ducks talk in tones
    of low strings breaking,
herding their young from shadow to shadow
as fox and coyote hunt the watery verge
and hawks swing between the day moon
    and dry, white sun,
their hunger patient, and penetrative as a
    ray of light.

Two years... Medicines, treatments, hopes
tidal in their lift and fall, and at all times
the fated slide towards the fire
however we mate or pay to drug ourselves
    with the latest wonder—
why shouldn't age greet death instead as
    Friend,
have you come to end my suffering?

Tomorrow storm will again whiten the hollows
     between the groves,
whiten the leaves, whiten the sky, whiten
the air with slashes of cold, pale rain
however my heart hungers for summer
     like a fire under snow.
No wonder I yearn for purpose
as clear as coyote or fox or hawk

who set hunger on foot or give it wing,
but I am left just words for loss, for lateness,
     for the late blooming of relief,
words that matter, sure, and promise an end
or give a shape to hope, yet are not enough,
not flesh not bone but air in my mouth
     absence in my belly

coals in my brain.

SOFT WEATHERS

I lived my father's long dying
spread-eagled in the bog through a two year
    winter:
sleet-slashed, sleeked by frozen rain
I gleamed in the cold light in primary hues,

all that time unable to move,
grief layered in snowfall on fall,
covered by floodtide for months, still
still except for the slow ooze of mud

embracing my flesh before, finally,
spring's ebbtide bared me, stunned,
    to this sun.
I sit up as the cranberry beds
lift through the ebb,

blink in the light, dazed, unsteady
    when I stand,
and wash in the stream,
cross naked to firmer land
where the oaks are new leaved with suns,

gay streamers hanging from their boughs.
I feel grass in my toes, and smell
its hayscent where mown, taste
the musky pink vulva of lady slippers

inviting me to dim recesses—
I forgot so much, giving my senses to my
    father…
My face opens in this light,
lianas of paradise flowers entwine my arms,

rugosa roses thicket my legs. My tongue
croaks like a crow from a height,
loosens, speaks winds in a whoosh of wings,
speaks— god knows— of the forgetting
    in renewal,

of the loss of what seemed beyond loss
that turns out, in this heat-drugged air
to be something I can't even name:
speaks as though I spoke

warm light   clear skies   soft weathers...

PEACE

Alpine meadow... A brook spills over stones
to merge far below with the ocean-bound,
gray-green glacial Adige.

Near peaks shake off their covers
and yawn toothily in the sun,
gleaming like new-polished lanceheads.
I burn aware with them, coughing,

sip water coldly pure as a knife in my lungs,
free at last to be ill, in myself, recover, be well,
the duties due the dying, well done...

Each to its own— death, mountain, brook,
a man alive to climb   to fall   and again work uphill
to the high place where the waters start to gather
the deep peace of the sea.

CONTRASEASONS

Autumn
Spring
Summer
Winter

AUTUMN

A greater surf pounds the beach— dawns
    grow cold, and evenings:
one morning a last crescent of day moon
    hangs north of the sun,
      and the season falls tartly on the tongue.
Austerities of bright space flood the East;
    metallic sunsets burn the West—
one noon the sea wears the thin, brief glitter
    of a mayfly's wing,
the air silent as those brilliant daubs of color
    that buzzed and clicked and lately fiddled
vanish into the ground...

Cranberries sheet the flooded bogs red, then oak
    and maple steal their hues and smolder
      among the pines,
to catch fire like matches in a row
    under skies defining emptiness. Storm clouds
tangle in the trees, snuffing their fire, or
    whirl upward in steaming flames:
when the gray clears, limbs startled bare
scratch winter from the sky— while wind
sweeps away the bright mosaics a
    careless artist laid on the roads
with the deep theme of time's passage, and how
    that passage is beautiful.

The last ducks and geese quawk and honk as
      they lift and leave when
the great wave that rolls up the beach and punches
      through the dunes to resalt the moors
hustles autumn into winter, resounding.
We grow afraid of death, white as the winter sky
      at noon, as the breath that runs before us,
            as the ice that held this land in its fist;
of being where all that is, is stark and bare as bone
      nearly stone,
of being old, of wanting without will, and knowing
      ourselves so.

All these draw me from the city of burning
      suns beside the numb Pacific
to stand on native ground and recall
      in lymph and marrow
what gives our hearts the power to go on—
a reality learned first, and deepest, of
      even light, of neither dead cold nor
            thoughtless warmth,
of words that soothe, arms that reassure, and
      the smile that gives winter its lie
            at the doorway to the world.

SPRING

A cold wind blows waxwings through
    calligraphies of winter brush: they are
      old autumn leaves, dun and sear,
with flashes of memory's brilliant reds
      on their wings.
A season's arrested growth of beard stubbles
    underfoot, thin skeins
      of ice brittle as old men's
        skin over the pools—
yet there a robin stalks a pond's frozen lip,
    on fire.

Geese pause on the river, splash upwards
    and V north over trees
      where starlings cluster, impatient as
        ill men to be well,
as all men who hunger to be free of the
      cold distance of discomfort
    their drudgery exiles them to:
they ignore the small woodpeckers carrying
      coals on their heads,
like me anxiety each sleepless 4 am.

All is mixed in all, on edge,
    polar wastes and ruined leftovers
      with intimations of new lives:
even the coldest wind burns,
    and no chill is deeper than on
      a summer's day
        or the thought of loss while in
    a woman's arms.

We wait to be young again, patient
          as a clenched jaw
as buds burn yellow and red prints on the
      winter sky
   and green flames twist through the ice,
not wise, not choosing all, but enduring,
as though punished for some sin past recall.

We shudder, and the ground, whose great
     brown wings beat through scribbled stars—
only yesterday they carried me from the light,
               but now
           because they must
        because forgiveness, too, is in
      the nature of things,
they bring me closer and closer to the flame.

SUMMER

Summer is the post-coital moment
    of surfeit that leaves a taste of ashes
        on the tongue—
when behind the blaze of days
    the sun almost forgets to dim
        the year starts to decline
and all moves towards a ripeness
    we must devour to relieve—
        corn that ripens within its silks,
the fattening thighs of roots in earth,
    melons full-breasted on their vines,
        tomatoes who burst their skins,
then drip on their leaves:

when newmown hay rots in the sun,
    the sweet stench half pleasing
        like low tidal flats under the
midday broil, or red dulse abandoned on
    the high tide line; when heat
        lifts acrid whiffs of ocean
from dune sand and grass, the sand
    pillowy underfoot that in winter was
        bare and firm, the grass matted
that was thin: when bees fly drunk
    from nectar turned hard in its sac,
        and insects whine and buzz and click
dry cantatas in humid air
    to celebrate another day's survival
        after morning swallows mob their
dazed struggle to rise on damp, sheer wings.

Night grows out of the ground
    in slow, black flowers that open together:
        clouds thicken, secretive as fertile women—
then large soft drops slide from the leaves,
    bemused and wobbling.
        This is the season Adam fell, and Eve
that seems it cannot end,
    when bad air in the cities
        badly mimics marsh miasma and decay,
and sweat and ripening, racking lust
    become a brilliant nightmare—
        when tears sweeten sorrow with their salt
and we wander in a daze from feast to feast,
    gunshot breaks of boughs
        bent by fruit grown profuse
disturbing the night:
    when our hearts hear the year say
        I am the body of eternity—
come, eat...

So summer dominates us all,
    reductive, tyrannical, in velvet boots,
        refusing all offers to surrender,
promoting the party line until the end.
    One day, we wake like a man
        in a field a storm we slept through
laid waste—
    the air is cold, the sky sanded bare,
        and we remember
how ardently we deceived ourselves
    thinking   *If   if only   if*
        we said to a perfect day,   *stay*
it would...

Orion climbs into the night,
   a club in one hand,
      running his hounds past harvest past
stubble into the season
   when my heart becomes a stag
      leaping towards colder days.
We remember our dreams with regret
   and hunger to be lean, to relearn
      the meaning of completion
through the hunger at our heels...
   It is this wanting too much,
      this wanting built into our hearts
that brings the lightning down
   that sets our sere flesh aflame
      like a field we must fire
to nourish another year with ashes.

WINTER

Now death slips into thought and dream
as easily as slumber in my too warm room,
for spring and summer have run
from the shattered jails of the woods,
and my fear all could be stripped
    has come true.

Deer dun as bark or black as shadows on
    new-fallen snow
quiver and stare as silence gathers and ice
matches the lakes' eyes to the sky's white,
while my heart shivers in its cage of bones
exposed as the cardinal in naked woods.

    Go down and become nothing,
        feel hope fail, let go the fever
    that fuels the mind with want; I will go
        into the dark with acid on my tongue,
    grief past tears or words, past even
        the repair of the womb,
    and feel the emptiness of all efforts
        to save those you love.
    Say All I have done, all
        known, all thought to store
    against loss, is futile—
        and let that go too, tasting the
    last bitterness of forgetting.

But what of the heart's and the veins'
    living lava cased
in cold silver finning iced-over depths?
Of life pending in sac and egg or
wrapped in winter silks on winter limbs
though the countless shining wings that
    fed the day

or the crawling things that filled the shadows
    with dread, are gone?
The pond's ice pens spring's thunder
    in its hold, crackling
like lightning as it tightens its grasp,
booming some nights under alert stars
that have rubbed summer's sleep
    from their eyes.

Blue spruce and green fir flare
over summer's smother; ice that sheathes
    the woods all one night
sprays beauty from countless prisms
    in the morning:
by evening snow flashes into being
like fireflies who brighten June evenings,

each flake unique as each of the dreams
that flock together in our minds
    for warmth... In cities
calligraphies of new plays envine marquees
while paintings leaf from gallery walls
and things and things and more
    pile up in windows where passersbys

and children press as though these were
corn and wheat and round harvest
    ripenesses.
All want to say *Death has no being*—
though nature is not here or there but where
we stand: what flesh can lose, it will,
    and so spirit, too.

What then does the world mean,
    speaking *winter*? That question
rowels our hearts with its spurs
and the answer we guess even more
whether days are long or nights longer—
the word winter speaks is *love*,

one that contains all of desire and fear,
where we rank no higher than dust
that one day will be part of something
    that lives— one warm morning
penned thunder breaks free from the ice,
and depths that were gray gleam blue

as a clear high noon: what was frozen
in rigor mortis grows supple as pure
energy fuses up from the root where
we sank to find what would be left of
ourselves stripped to the core, now happy

as the first man when the world was new.

ROMAN POEMS

RIVER OF FLESH

homage to Auden

I came to see the Dome
    and the curved embrace of stone
        that gathers in the faithful
to St. Peter and his tomb; to see
    the catacombs where martyrs lie,
        and the Sistine where
Michelangelo made
God in our image—

instead I heard a crowd shout, not men, not women
    but sheets of loud color urging lion and tiger
        to rend believers with fang and claw,
or chariots to run them under hoof and wheel
    and scythe those left standing on either side.
        A quarter million roared as those who still stood or
crawled were hacked or shot or hauled away and gassed
    while vultures merged into a single shadow
        above the blood and stiffening gore.

I came to see the Forum's ruins
    once brilliant in the sun,
        to walk where the sacred fire burned
and kings bowed to free men
    whose words gave life or death:
        to see where Caesar burned
and Antony fired the crowd
to grief— all safely passed—

instead a lonely Asian tourist asked me by
　　anonymous ruins, "Where is Caesar buried?"
　　　　I sent him to the Forum, and left a
laurel bough in the grit and gloom of a basement
　　built where once he twitched his robe over his wounds.
　　　　Tourists lowed before the nearby Pantheon
where Italy's exiled kings lie in place of Jove and Mars,
　　or Venus who might have brought love's fist
　　　　to this flash-filled, loveless space.

I stood before St. Theresa
　　to see her body convulse
　　　　in God's embrace:
to see Christ in supple stone
　　grace his mother's lap,
　　　　and St. Peter's chains aglow
as though he was never crucified,
head down—

instead a mass filled the street in every era's dress:
　　I rubbed my eyes certain I was asleep,
　　　　but they remained when I dropped my hands
and gathered me in. Under a sky burning to coal I
　　groaned as they groaned,
　　　　begged as they begged
for water to ease my thirst, but no help came
　　in all the time it took the buildings to fall into ruin
　　　　under a sky raining hot ash.

I came to see fountains spray,
    the four rivers stream
        in Piazza Navona, Saldi's
rising figures in the Trevi, the
    Triton blowing his conch near
        Via Veneto: to see lovers
take pictures to recall they
stood there, young, joyous—

instead I saw the generations fill the Tiber,
    my own face rise and sink among the others
        with dull or astonished or hopeless eyes,
and all those I love and all they will love and those too
    in that river of flesh flowing past Castel Sant' Angelo
        towards the sea where all roads end
and all times meet, where striving follows striving,
    thirst thirst, dream dream
        we never waken from, or slake, or gain.

                                        Rome, 2009

BERNINI DEFENDS HIS ECSTASY OF ST. THERESA AGAINST CHARGES OF CARNALITY

"Why mock Theresa's head thrown back,
   lips parted, body helpless with pleasure—
or laugh at the angel with an arrow
   hovering like a refined cupid
certain of the target? Or at the spray of gold
   to show God's grace entering the saint-to-be,
and her visionary ascent to His arms?
   How should I celebrate the soul embraced
and reunited with its source? the mingling of
   divinity and dust? With ashes in her hair,
charcoal on her tongue, rags in place of the
   passionate flutter of her robes, sores
to mar a face of perfect, ardent marble?
   What alternative does a woman have
to ecstasy in such a complete embrace
   but convulsions of joy, her tears far from grief?
We know beauty begins with the flesh
   but hope for a love that shows contempt for
the years, even dreams of defying death.
   I wanted still more, the pure transcendence of
self in that Other who stands before and
   after time whom our yearning, if nothing else,
makes real! So I caught Theresa as she blurs
   into her dream's sun, a woman lost to all
but the ending of her emptiness, loneliness,
   childlessness... See if you compose yourself
so those untouched won't laugh when you
   are transported to a greater being. You will do

as she did: let yourself go utterly and pray
    from your loneliness in that moment
ultimate love makes you burn and beg,
    'Take me. Take everything.'"

GRAFFITI IN THE UNDERWORLD

nothing human is alien to me.... Terence

One midnight past my middle years
    with slow steps   dulled eyes
I drift across Rome's cobblestoned streets
    busy with tourists by day down
to its underworld, tired of life,
    love become rote gesture...
Fluorescent light fills the landing
    and fades into tunnels on either side,
but no trains come, no one joins me,
    not even ghosts to beg for blood
for an hour's life. Stillness reigns...
    I find spray paint in my hand,
a knife on my belt: I wear black,
    thick-soled boots, black leather
pants and a vest nail-head studded,
    chained-looped: bewildered,
my hand is orange from rubbing
    my spiked hair, and as I flex
my biceps a man's pelvis spears between
    a woman's legs. The walls writhe
with life, great blocks of letters march
    their length, crude epithets and
epigrams snake above and below
    mixed with scenes of women
who ride men like bulls, their cunts
    hungry mouths. Caesar is lampooned
for a penis too big for Brutus' mother,
    Servilia, to mouth; pot-bellied

Berlusconi without corset and suit runs
    from the horns his wife holds
towards Leticia, a Lolita who eggs him on
    as she flees with a backward leer...
Dazed, I spray scenes of my own
    in this two-thousand year old jumble
as crowds pour in from the tunnels
    and sweep me up to ravish   rob
strip   choke   stab   shoot   raw
    pleasure all, and all pleasures one.

Lost, appalled, I become a heap of rags
    stinking, homeless, abandoned,
        abandoning
until in the cold hour before dawn
    I stagger home, a junkie coming
off a bad trip, creep in my door,
    shower, slip into bed— and lie awake,
trying, unable to, forget.
    Dawn spills its water across the floor...
I pretend to be myself when I stumble
    down to eat   to plan another day of
fountain to statue to column to ruin
    taking pictures of the bright world
as though there is no other to record.
    But as days and weeks pass
I see openings to that raw underlife
    where I feel my heart feed in the
red darknesses that pulse in my flesh—
    danger makes my blood beat
as strongly as any shared passion,
    unable to tell pain from pleasure:
and danger gives my tenderness
    its poignance and love its power

to hold the blood's ravings within—
    for my step regains its spring,
my eyes the light they lost
    and love is renewed with her who
these many years keeps me warm
    however I age or stray in the night.

GIORDANO BRUNO STEPS DOWN
FROM HIS PEDESTAL IN THE HEAT

with the grind and scrape
of bronze robes, hood swept
back with a thud, and wipes
sweat melting from his cheeks
with a heavy sleeve.
                              Romans
and tourists overturn flower
vases, household goods, and
food stalls in their rush from
Campo de' Fiori. Giordano sees me
hold my ground, and shrugs.
They always run. His voice is
the scrape of rusted hinges:
*It's hard to stand when the sun
is summer in spring,* he adds,
*I feel fires lick my flesh again and
blind my eyes. That's how I died.*
He points at the pedestal.
*They piled wood around a stake
there and set it on fire, the crowd
raw with pleasure from my torment.
Another age covered the ashes
with this stone— those bastards
who burned me should see me
now, honored, statued.*

He walks through the stalls
towards a tall spigot of running
water, robes flapping as though
already sodden, bends, and
sprays himself. Water steams

from his body, his head
he douses to still the heatwaves
visible even in this light. *Still here?*
I nod, mute, as his steam thins
in the air. *They wait 'til I remount*
before they return to their stalls—
no one says a thing.
Something hollow laughs
Who would believe them?
Statues don't walk around
Campo de' Fiori— what a
heat-addled, mass delusion!

He strolls back to the pedestal,
surrounded by bronze plaques
that show him as teacher,
defendant, burning martyr.
I said, The round world goes
round a round sun, the cosmos
His wheel He binds us on:
at the root lies what we cannot
divide or destroy, quanta, in
your lingo, or strings, each
tuned to one special note
in His mind that together make
an earthly and divine music—
that flower there, or knife fallen
on the ground, the desert stone
and rain, hawk and prey, Gypsy,
Jew, terrorist, child blown apart,
each broken limb
                    are symphonies
that bind His fire to shape and
sense, each thing Him, sacred,

equally divine. I said, The mind
finds nothing opposed to Him.
They burned me for that.
They wanted Him a cleric
chanting matins at dawn, safe,
never to be probed or challenged,
or for us to grow or change
or face His danger or learn
this song He sings of Himself.

He remounts his pedestal,
flips his hood gray and green
with age over his face.
The Campo teems with life...
A vision then, delusive,
heat-addled, but I grow cold
as the blue sky peels away
and starfield on field opens
to view, each wheeling
across the sky faster than
the last, until the final whirl
of stars blurs into one light
holding all notes in one chord
I guess as though I near a
concert hall and imagine
the piece playing inside.
He laughs heavily... The sky
blues, brilliant: I hold
my hands up and see
my fingers are flames.
Welcome to the real, grinds
in my mind: *look at me, at how*
I burn in this music still.

TIVOLI

How did I come to this height where
rain slathers down and binds the steep,
gray sky to the blood-soaked plains
no amount of water can clean,
only grow more richly?

Through the graffitied
underworld into the land's
green glare, snaking
towards Tivoli whose
waters stream and fall...

I remember...
                    We escaped to a hillside
park of fountains, sprays greater than
Rome's set among pools and grottoes:
clouds merged and cooled and threw
drop down after drop.

A week juggling the ages
in Rome was enough.
I see my breath in the
cool air, and think:
I'm here.

When the sun beats on the wet wheat,
soaked walls, silvered roads, will mist
make the earth look like an Eden
for me and the woman beside me
to enter, be renewed, begin history again?

Silence... then fresh rain
taps the ground.
I see my breath in the
cool air, and think:
I am...

No...
      I will go into the earth, merge
with the rain, grow or shrivel
as the season demands:
lover, husband, grandfather, poet,
let my life pass like clear, swift waters.

NO ONE COMES FOR PENELOPE—

The Wayfarer
The Raveled Woman, Earlier
The Battered Man
Dreams
Collision
Find Me
The Shadow And The Son
The Way Home

The end of the *Odyssey* or the end of the former asylum in Camarillo, California, mirrors in mirrors—

with the complete artwork of Ron Sandford…

THE WAYFARER

His name is Robbery Rodman,
not the best for a man

who tries to take delusions
that fill lifetimes

from those with nothing
to take their place.

But— always that word:
to help others to the real!

What a godlike gift
to call a world into being

where before
there was no more

than a mirage.
Worth all frustration,

he thinks as the fields
pile up like dirt

a tractor banks,
"Some trick of the light,"

he mutters, and steps on it
so the dark Mercedes

arrows towards the asylum,
deadlines instead of

headlines in his head,
budget cuts to come,

mental healthcare
pared to hands just stubs,

all but the violent
to be turned loose.

"They will gibber
on streetcorners,

flocks of something
we think we know

whose looks
will turn us cold."

Three he hopes
to break the rules for by

throwing them together,
their delusions so alike

he will explode them,
like atoms in a collider

with each other's madness,
not private but shared,

no current but reality
needed for the shock,

not to arch their spines
or convulse their flesh

or set spittle drooling
but to break into

their attention with
their own desperate need:

to make them recoil
into this world—

maybe—

he brushes doubt aside,
reminds himself

desperate times
call for like measures

to lead them towards
the real sun, earth, wind

off the near Pacific—
to the truth, that pearl—

he catches himself—
that plainest of stones

once part of a burning sea,
or molten river when

everything was young,
until after what upheavals

refined to a small
smooth shape lifted

from the shore,
so simple, so full

of meaning. An adage
floats into mind,

"Things do not change, we do"
though it does not follow.

"There..." The asylum
lifts from the fields,

its white buildings wings
folded between low hills,

mountains rising beyond,
brown now, soon purple,

soon October, so far
from spring...

THE RAVELED WOMAN, EARLIER

A menace shapes in the far corner
   and swells as it moves across the floor
     like something with one bad leg
   it drags behind the good
but no face no limbs, a rod

   of darkness alone, herself aware
in her dream that she dreams,
   desperate to wake then awake,

her room a reel of shadows,
   her tapestry blows as though
in a breeze, then stills, raveled

   threads dangle, the promise
to wed when done undone each night.
   They let me, better a prize for all

than one to make all losers,
   better a kiss stolen in a hallway,
a rough hand between my legs,

   my dress lifted like a serving girl's,
my gasp inflaming an ear
   but no more! she thinks, and relives

those touches that build torment
   until a single touch makes her
frantic to finish alone on her bed

as she had earlier, then tore at the
tapestry until she could breathe again:
   now she wills herself to sleep

again the menace drags towards her
   again she swims up from her dream
again awake gasps gulfs of air,

      an incomplete woman who tears
   at herself by night and by day hides
her loose threads from the men,
      unable to close her eyes until at dawn
      she plunges into dreamlessness.

THE BATTERED MAN

He sponges off the gore and blood,
　　the suitors a tumble of red rags
　　in his hall, the last screams
of slaughtered women who solaced

　　their lust knives to his ears.
　　He shrugs on a fresh tunic,

catches his son's eye, who nods,
　　clean in turn— *I was slender*
　　steel like him fresh-oiled, gleaming;
she won't like my first lesson taught him

　　to kill and kill until none live.
　　A kaleidoscope twists in his mind—

　　an arrow with a pop and squelch
　　　　burrows into an eye;
　　a spear shuttles death, stopped
　　　　by an "Unh!" as a man topples;
　　a sword thrusts down a throat's
　　　　pink vulva as legs
　　jerk like a woman coming,
　　　　making death an obscenity—
　　all with the mingled roars
　　　　of challenge and fearful cries
　　and death rattles, then just
　　　　death's look, fish scales
　　grown dull out of water.

Whatever we do to others comes home
   to us, he thinks, and starts
   from his son's touch, his boy
no boy but as much a man as he

   when he walked to the quay,
   stepped aboard and gave the order

to bear away, eyes fixed forward...
   Yet there is still farther to go...
   Will she know me my fingernails
scraped clean as a butcher's

   with a lifetime's cleaving to wash off?
   His eyes, then feral as a hawk's,

free of mercy, are now just tired,
   a man who has seen too much.
   He drags his weight into a headwind
the last length of corridor towards her

   as though led against his will,
   his hunger a lead weight on his heart.

DREAMS

First looks... In a flash he:
                        tired rings
   below her eyes, a bad night, years
     of bad nights,

I'm no fool, I feel her grief, her anger...
   How tall she is, straight, eyes level
     with mine, how could I forget?

The child-woman who made herself short
   is gone. Her hair is long, its auburn and gold
     highlights transport him—

   the sun sets in a red-gold haze
     as a man with a black mane
   lunges under his shield—
     he drops his hard,
   snaps the man's spear,
     knocks him off balance,
   his sword drives into his neck
     the man gurgles the man dies
   in that redgold light—
     warriors
   draw apart, clash swords
     clash shields, acclaim him— .

He tears his eyes from her hair,
   takes in her straight nose, full lips,
     compressed, no quiver, eyes steady

I am a maimed thing against her beauty!
    And she:
                I forgot I am as tall as this stranger,
    nose broken, some Trojan blow,

death is in his eyes though she puzzles
    a wisdom there— *after all he lives, is here,*
      alone of all those who brushed us aside

to see new lands do savage things
    to other men and women.
      She takes in his scarred arms,

thickened body and shoulders,
    a man ragged as a robe
      some madman or rough lover tore

some girl begs her to replace
    and wonders if he is worth mending.
      "I tried to stay."

His voice is strange, too.
    Though her reproaches hang on her lips
      like snow piled on a high slope

ready to sweep all away,
    all she says is
             "You left."
    "I hid in the fields I plowed

like a slave until they found me."
  "You left."
    "All left, every king, every warlord,

else they would have burned us
  before they burned Troy.
    I had no choice."

"You, left!"
  He senses he cannot win this.
    "Who are you?"

What does he have
  to give her, a world wonder of a sack
    and treasure hoard he lost?

He never cared about those,
  he wanted respect, wanted
    to be done, he used his mind

to be free, and for all that wandered
  as long again, ships lost, men, lost— .
    Some god hated me! he tells himself,

but he no longer believes in any god.
  The day's images flood his mind—
    I left her to a hall of men like bad meat.

"Show me the scar."
  He bares where the tusk tore his thigh
    the memory alive in his eyes—

the boar eludes his spear
and gouges his flesh as he
turns just enough to live,
sword out he sinks in the pig
full length, then rolls away
from its death throes— .

Lightly she touches the white line
and steps away.
"So. It is you."

Dully he stares at the tapestry,
a slab of beef who passed inspection,
then focuses on the scenes woven there—

First he plunges his sword
in the boar, next stands
behind a plow, surrounded
by armored men,
flocks of gulls overhead:
then sees his ships
as their doomed crews bend
their backs to the oars
on a windless dawn—
a winedark sea is touched red
on another as they grind
onto Troy's beach.
Men strain against men
in a crush of shields and spears
under a black rain of arrows
and a splintered sun:

a red pool mingles the fires
　　of burning Troy
and a horse whose skeleton
　　is tongued by flames.
His eyes move to himself
　　lying as though drugged
on a strange shore,
　　exhausted men around him
lost to their dreams—
　　then see his men harpooned
from a ship in a narrow strait
　　he sailed too near a cliff.
The great whirlpool swirls
　　where he lost hope yet sailed by,
and where, strapped to the mast,
　　he listens to women sing
with faces past beauty
　　but claws under their wings,
Take me from despair and death
　　stitched to his mouth.
He sees the cave's trap,
　　the cannibal huge with
his single urge to eat them,
　　as though one-eyed,
I blinded him, said I was
　　No One
he cursed me.
　　His men stare beastially
at a woman he pumps
　　remorselessly...

There is the other
     who offered endless love,
as if that could exist...
     The images rush together—
the last girl so ripe, so
     virginal, so torn by
teen-age lust
     for the famous man,
then grief when he sailed,
     so certain to forget him
utterly.
     Stunned, he sees men
feasting in his hall
     lie next in their blood,
last how threads dangle
     from their own shapes.
How he went to hell
     is missing, unless,
he realizes with a start,
     that is what these images
show: how a man
     deep into killing
sits down with Death
     and calls him friend,
blood in his cup
     to let him speak...

"These were my dreams. I wove them there."
     "They are my life, all true."
          "My dreams always are.

And become nightmare."
   Doubt floods, he hears the curse
      "No One you are No One you will be!"

not sworn as he thought at the cave
   but at his birth.
      The floor opens beneath him

he plunges downward in fear
   he is locked in a room where
      he fights someone else's shadows...

COLLISION

He imagines the room take shape,
   white walls where a thin body pounds
      his head against the pads, dazed

muttering to himself, his son in a white
   thing with his arms tied in back:
      a woman with dull brown hair

stands by a bare bed staring at him,
   confused, the same phrase on her lips,
      "Who are you *are you*?" her eyes

moving between himself and a blank place
   where no tapestry stands. A seated man
      in dark clothes rustles papers on his lap.

"Now is your chance
to grasp the real

before they close this
place down and toss

you on the street," he says—
"that's their plan, there is

no more money
no more patience

no more care for you,—
for all they care

you three can dream
your lives away

beneath an underpass
in a cardboard box

as traffic overhead
shakes the ground and

rains dust on your
louse-filled hair— ."

His tone is a raven's
croak beside his ear.

"You must choose.
The end has come."

The man's eyes meet Robbery's,
troubled, lucid:

Robbery trembles.
"Why do I care

you wonder?
What a rare chance

for change you three offer:
if one wakes, maybe

he can shock another free—
speak to her!

Speak to him!
This chance will not repeat!"

"My years," he mutters—
"All lost. All dream."

He stares at the dark man,
   imagines being other than he is,
      a complete stranger to his life

dragging these in his wake,
   calling all he has been and done
      a poverty, a waste of dreams,

while a world waits where he would be
   a latecomer to the race,
      with no chance to catch more

than a laggard or two,
   in every sense, no one— —
      and even so, better off— — .

He steadies himself against the wall
   as the floor rocks, grabs the boy,
      who stares at him, his pounding stilled,

eyes fearful—
   while the panic in the woman's
      breaks his heart. He lets the boy go,

who hangs on his words:
   No, no no. He finds his tongue: "No"
      and shakes himself,

"You are the dream,
   the nightmare,
      the doubt in my heart

to break my will,
   the dark shape of my despair
      always trying to escape

the cave where I blinded you
   to where I stand to steal my sight."
      He stares across the floor:

it steadies: lifts his eyes:
   the tapestry firms, padded walls, man,
      and boy disappear...

They are alone, the proud woman, and man...
   This was the worst: not Circe, not Calypso,
      not lost lives, lost years, spilled blood:

this doubt, this despair at this door.
   The silence hums between them
      pregnant with unspoken words,

with passion,
   with a quiver in the flesh:
      with hope.

FIND ME

He stares again at the tapestry and knows
    what is wrong: *nothing of her is there.*
        He meets her eyes even

as he takes in her hair's living gleams.
    "I have not lived eighteen years.
        What would I say, what weave?"

she answers his look, and knows then
    why the great pour of words has not come.
        "The bed—"

"Carved from a living tree, rooted there."
    "The only roots here...
        I dream of you—

you are a black thing that drags towards me
    I try to escape even asleep."
        Can this get worse? he wonders, then

how much he must pay—
    "You will never be done."
        "You can still read my mind."

He knows then they are one
    to endure, one to do,
        the extreme of every husband and wife.

He sits on the bed.
    "We must somehow start again.
        I meant myself to be my gift,

what else do I have? A fool's thought,
   I know, it kept me going,
     force I knew was nothing,

wisdom I learned is nothing,
   illusion fed me but is nothing.
     I thought I had come here

with nothing else— but that too is wrong,
   I am not empty-handed, wife."
     The word is honey, the word is

gall
   ashes
     vinegar

sugar—
        for a moment
  he cannot move his tongue.
    "I have a gift after all.

Teach me, Penelope— "
  he spends her name at last:
    "how to cry again."

Disembodied she sees herself sit by him
  and take a hand so unlike the one he slid
    up her thigh their wedding night.

"There is more."
           "There always is."
  "There's an oar I must take
    where no one knows its use."

Startling him, she laughs.
  "To me it is a shuttle for weaving
    on the loom of my life,

a needle to thread and finish— "
  a wave towards the tapestry:
    "I am the people

who do not know you,
  the girl wife mother
    courted abandoned

to a woven life in place of a real;
  I am your undiscovered land.
    Find me."

THE SHADOW AND THE SON

The house is silent, the cleaning is done,
the survivors silent in their rooms;
   the son stands outside the great door
   legs spread, shield on one arm, spear
held in the other.
               One by one they gather,
   fathers, uncles, brothers, cousins of the dead.
They keep their distance.
                 There will be
rent robes, mothers' howling, hands on weapons
   no one will draw: a rite, some animal's blood
   steams on an altar, blood for blood, blood
to cancel blood, blood is the world's money.
   Placated, they will go home.
   He has seen ruthless Helen endured
by her husband to keep her home
   so she does not set the land on fire again
   and plow men each spring into the ground
like her forbears plowed kings down
   to make the grain grow before
   the Greeks came with gods to marry
and master hers.
              No such woman for me
   but some sister to some man killed here,
   a peace offering, my life on this island,
plowing my fields, her body, no more.
   He hopes his father touches his mother,
   God knows she needs to be touched
while she still feels desire: in the end
   what we give makes us real, although
   it never matches the more we yearn for.

He is not bitter. He has lived too little,
   thought too much, you know the kind—
   "Silent waters run deep" they said when
he was a child. Now he has his desire, the family
   that never was. The sun sets in winter's colors,
   metallic reds layer by layer give way to
gold streaks, crossed swords in a burnished
   blue that scums to gray, red darkens
   to nightfall— torches sputter, flare,
burn brightly, gutter and flicker out
   like ourselves.
                    We will make peace
   when dawn's hues strengthen
until day is bright as a girl's jewels
   held to the sun: how beautiful that will be.
   He never asks when he forgot how to cry,
or to sleep except in short bursts, or to dream,
   only wonders if men have meaning
   or are sharks stirred now and then
to frenzied feeding, or wet wood
   that smolders and smokes until flames
   burst out and leave nothing behind: if
men hold only damages when they are done—
   last if god sees the world as beautiful, wars,
   lovers breathless in one another's arms,
an infant slaughtered, a hero on his pyre,
   a madman banging his head against a wall,
   all gems glowing in the divine crown—
and shrugs, the thought too difficult, and too
   strange. He has his father's shadow.
   He is content.

THE WAY HOME

The fields peel away,
discarded rinds as he speeds

from the asylum.
Throwing those three together

was the toss of loaded dice
certain to fail, he thinks wryly

now. *One shocked moment*
and then... He passes

fields with laborers
still bent to their work,

and suddenly pulls the
car to the shoulder.

A fog bank fingers
over the flat fields

from the near Pacific:
fifty yards away

in the misting light
the men and women

half crouch, half crawl
to pluck strawberries

from their secret places.
Illegals, from Mexico or...

doing what they must
to live so that Helen

can buy the fruit they pick
without idea or care

from where it comes,
no more than me...

He sees their kitchen,
newly retiled, the great

vintage stove refurbished,
imagines Helen's cool

acceptance of his return
from another well-paid

day of failure: accounts
race through his head,

bills for furnishings, for
clothes, for tuition for

his children who eat
the sweat of these even

more thoughtlessly than he...
He knows the sea

changes under these clouds
from bright to a winedark hue

these working do not see.
I could be by a field

three thousand years ago,
the same bent shapes

toil for my benefit,
the same superior, tired

indifference in my heart,
thinking ahead

to the evening meal
and entertainment,

some song about long
travels and travails,

no, something lighter
that makes light of all

that is dark. He recalls how
when the man in the asylum

drew the woman down
beside him on the bed,

her eyes grew alert
as he never once saw

in years of therapy:
how she must have

pulled my words apart
each night, like unraveling

a sleeve or hem.
He left them there,

private for the first time,
took the boy to another room,

shaken as he thought
they were better off

colluding in delusion...
Doubt strikes him

sudden as a snake
who has studied its prey

still, coiled, pent
then whips forward

fangs lowered,
venom pulsing, and

strikes—
just as I collude,

as anyone does
in shared lives

so normal to ourselves
so strange to others.

What does it matter
what I think when

there is really only
the one song,

a man and woman's
journey towards each other,

a homecoming always sought,
always later than we want,

always found on borrowed
time who paces across the years,

a shadow in clear light,
featureless in dream,

a heaviness that will seize
and at last stop my heart.

What value the real
when our lives are like

Helen on the phone,
"Did *he?*" "Did she?"

They, at least, dream greatly.
The man's voice echoes:

"You are the dream,
   the nightmare,
      the doubt in my heart

to break my will,
   the dark shape of my despair
      always trying to escape

the cave where I blinded you
   to where I stand
      to steal my sight."

He struggles for breath
as the workers move

in lengthening shadows
across the fields,

standing through twilight,
a faceless man

in a world so bare
it must be a bad dream—

Are they my dream?
Am I theirs? or

as his doubt bites bone:
Who is dreaming us?

Now a man seems to him
not an atom to smash

but a diamond's facet,
or a dimension, or

a universe, each
above, beside, under

entangled, enfolded
with each other

so where he begins
and another ends

can hardly be guessed—
as though the strange

and normal, alien
and familiar, this

and otherworldly
are doughs to knead

in a single loaf,
or each a note in

being's groundsong
intuited at the edge

of sound, each
man, each woman,

each different, each
a difference to treasure

each part of one
endlessly diverse whole.

Men, stars, stones
on the beach, past

present future reel
in his mind: he gasps

with hunger for size,
for shape, for meaning,

for any sense
of the truth

that does not recede
on the horizon as he nears,

sure only his life
is so much less

than it could be,
at sea, uncompassed,

with no way to find
true north or south,

wholly uncertain
of his way home—

or if that is even
where he wants to go.

HEARTSONGS

new poems

SLACKWATER

Two days of cold rain, and the Gray Lady
  trails her veils over the near hills, summer's
all-consuming light gone in spring's softer,
  an entire winter lost. Things startle
with their clarity in this kinder light, like red
  bougainvillea petals and their serrate white
and palest orange eyes, beautiful as a girl's
  who stops me with a glance. I thought
we changed, not rocks or seas or seasons
  that trail one another remorselessly,
but the world hurries by, no more able to say
  'It is' than me, 'I am' with nothing sure
beyond the moment of saying. Death,
  you are the moment a smile stays curved,
grief or joy in the face in the mirror, fixed,
  time, the color of the day, every shape, frozen,
slackwater between tides where no tides flow.
  Should I exult with the dawn, roar and revel
in the day, that they come? A night, a month,
  a year when nothing is lost? Love the night
with its dreamflood and the secret movements
  light lays bare? He who pulls a child from
carnage, takes a blow meant for an innocent—
  or raises his hand to strike— all that is,
while it is, if it is? Good and evil in such transience
  are evanescent as leaffall in a strong wind.
Let the Gray Lady nudge us into another season,
  any season the tide can reach, the heart bear.

BLOOD RHYTHM

Yesterday long tongues of granite
   once fluid and desperate to reach water
bared their frozen lengths on the shore—
   last night the tide buried them
under summer's sand to double the beach.
   We soak up the sun blind to any furies
tamed underfoot, just as we forget in turn
   the infancy, youth, and apogee that feel
all in all but are gone in the grasping.
   One day we recall we live on sand
and quarry older lives; one day recall
   those graces we took for granted...

Yesterday we gasped on the tide line
   when first we crawled from the sea's menace—
our blood still echoes its tides, as those
   the older tides of fire whose starry furnaces
forged every atom that became at last
   flesh and soul. We are so wound in nature
I find no boundary between inner and outer,
   us and others, me and you...
                     Today children
scream in summer's waves... May they
   stay ignorant of winter's rockribbed shore.
May they revel in youth's grace forever.

NETTLES

Nettles surprise my bare arm
    stinging long after I withdraw—
unlike my moods that come
    and go without warning
however I try to learn
    the shape of their meaning.
I am not master of my heart,
    a wood pigeon hiding
sweet flesh in the pruned twilights
    of poplars...
When rain silvers the leaves
    and all London falls asleep,
wounds sting my dreams
    from when I was too young
to name or give them shape
    yet whose stings formed my heart.
My eyes open in the dark.
    No twist or turn stills
the hammer in my chest... I know
    the names of other fears—
that circle we complete
    with a senile smile
with each loss of face and name
    as memory fades;
that heart whose rolling
    thunder sinks to silence,
that garden whose nettles
    no longer sting.

NIGHT RIDE, THUNDER, HEARTROLL, STARS OVER THE WHITE HORSE OF UFFINGTON

There, glowing, a white horse strides
   unbroken whether through raingray
      or sundazzled days
where it scars the chalky hill.
   Every night it rides the heights,
      ghostly whether seen and known
or alone, unknown, but there
   as is the great unknown
      our lives are etched on so briefly,
that unknown which I fear less
   than its knowledge that will come...
      My heart, once just assumed,
thuds in the plain dark
   as I twist to find somewhere
      I can rest in peace. Found,
I freeze even as those hooves
   tread tirelessly across the ghostly hill
      like my chest's mortal thunder
that past the edge of sound
   rolls through the night ever closer…
      Pass by, bright horse, or let me ride you
under the stars that flower
   then flicker fall and fade
      like my heart's throbs with dawn.

        …The White Horse of Uffington was etched
        in the chalk of the Berkshire Downs about
        1000 B.C.

NIGHT TALK

...the night talk of stone and plant...Tolkien

Stone and plant weigh the earth's change,
    water and land's, heat and cold's
        their words few, and halt,
like ours when we suffer
    unwanted cruelty and change
        we cannot control or understand.
Heat hung on into November
    despite the early gale that stripped
        some trees bare among
the late confused still green.

When at last the cold wind blows
    and burns what's left
        to brown and russet red,
stone says to plant
    "See, it was only a passing fever"
        and plant to stone,
while sap struggles late to the root,
    "You have too much patience.
        It is worse year by year."
Again the loggerheads stay too long

in warm Cape Cod winds and waves,
    until the sudden winter cold
        strands them, stunned to bricks
on long bay beaches,
    their pulse fallen to one throb a minute.
        There we gather and swaddle
box and ship them
    to Carolina waters, a small atonement
        for all the damage we do.
Some say ours is not an age of blood

where innocents are not daily violated
    by violent men,
        but one where general happiness is
oh, so close.
    Then I hear plant and stone debate
        and the silence of the earth
which bears both our damage
    and the bodies of our innocents
        as it meditates its response,
and grow afraid.

RED IN TOOTH AND CLAW

Look how the young dolphin
    rolls in the wavewash,
shark-slashed head and body,
    spilled guts so fresh
they smudge the sand red.
    Surfers crest the near breakers
and a knot of children play
    farther down the beach
as the sun burns off the fog
    and emeralds the waves:
when he is found no one
    stops to say a final word.

      How far we have come
      from a life lived red
      in tooth and claw.

See him swim a moment ago
    alone, dappled by light
as kelp leaves brush
    against the sun
when stunned by a blow
    teeth slice off his cheek
then with one flail rip him
    throat to tail, his blood
hot in the shark's mouth.
    Late, too late, his family
torpedoes to save him—
    see them bear him up
until his eyes glaze, then
    surrender him to the tide...

How far we have come
from a life lived red
in tooth and claw…

Yesterday we marked
    the massacre at Srebenica,
bloodletting in Homs
    and Aleppo, the dying
in Kobani, the river of death
    in Rwanda. A ceremony
marked Katyn, Auschwitz
    was toured, a mass said
at Verdun, photos posed
    at Gettysburg, pyramids
of remembrances heaped
    as ambulances raced to
the Newtown schoolroom
    where blood will always
spill across the floor.

How far we have come
from a life lived red
in tooth and claw…

ASHES

Red skies over Napa   red skies over England
  then they redden over Portugal:
will Los Angeles' fires brown the Pacific's blues
  and rise over Japan?
                    Sparks large as silver dollars
rained upwards once from our near ridge—
  we almost fled our home. Tornadoes of flame
raced over Laguna's hills faster than flight,
  and one winter fire spread root to root in Alaska
until stopped by a hundred mile ditch delved
  below the snow. Once another snow fell
through a summer night from a pallid sky:
  ash coated streets and homes, whitened cars,
rose in puffs with our steps
  and left an odd fleshly residue
between our fingers from nearby Dachau.

I thought how the world burns, or we do
with a greater violence because we are who we are—
  though just now stars are visible in a clear sky
as persimmons orange in their green cradles
  and wisteria seeds startle as they snap
like birds hitting glass in this warm October night.
  What would it be to embrace, not destroy?
Would we be like the birds
  who shake themselves again into flight?
No, I think we are more like seeds
  who must be thrust down to rise into the light—
most of all those whose husks only fire splits
  so they may change our ashen lands to green.

BEES

Bees mob the flowering trees here on Hartzell, they hum
    as they hummed in the pines and flowers on Mt. Hymettus
in the long-gone days of Athen's glory, and down the years
    by their millions before.
                        Their hum is the dynamo's hum
that sends its current to my home where it changes to light
    to heat   so I may live, though it is not so sweet as honey.
Bee, dynamo, current, ourselves. We are all in nature,
    a city no less than a beaver's dam or an anthill
but built the way each of us can. I do what I must though,
    antlike, I do not know fully what I do. But we grow wild
as lichen that covers leaf and limb, mountain, desert, heights
    and depths, that threatens to be all in all: we are nature's
        cancer.
High on a night hill I hear Los Angeles' hum. Look how
    its myriad lights push ever outward to banish darkness.
Far waters slake its thirst, far dams course their power here
    though they fill with silt and spent rivers grow shallow
and sink into the earth.
                    No matter. We go farther.
    We take ever more that needs more, until at the end
        of ends
we will take ourselves. Imagine
    then how beehum fills a cleaner air. Imagine
how the bees' survive by dancing down the years
    the paths to secret yet open nectars. Imagine
then from a high hill how night spreads unbroken
    as far as any eye can see. Imagine,
last,
    how still that air is, how quiet the gloom
but for the eerie hum of silence in a wild, wary ear.

THE WORLD IS DYING

We kill coyotes in hundreds
in wood and bog, and now
    our seals so sharks who take
no more than they need

    will go away. We recoil
at nature's tooth and claw,
    yet no animal kills and kills
and kills even without knowing
    he kills like we kill

    and now the world is dying.

    All night the spring wind
pours through pine barrens
    and oaks and maples bare
of leaf, buds barely past winter:
    this summer there will be

fewer myriad crystal wings
    to click and buzz or chirrup
through the night: fewer yips
    and yowls in wood and bog,

fewer featherflutters to hunt
    the air or make it amorous.
All hide from us whether
    they burrow or run or fly
or dive to lightless depths

    for the world is dying.

One summer the last woman
and last child will hear the wind
   pour through skeletal pines
shorn of needles; through oaks

   and maples barren of bud,
and see nothing fly or burrow
   or stalk or swim however
she may cry in loneliness,
   or, if silent, sit like a stone

with a stone for her heart
   and a stone cold child
in her arms. Great thoughts
   crumble with the books,

even silicon memories fail
   when a thousand years hit
Erase.
   We will be forgotten.
Grain by grain the salt wind

   will change woman and child
to a column of salt until rain
   dissolves and washes away even
the human stain from the earth

   for the world is dying.

Cape Cod, 2019

A NEW SEASON

Cold. Warm. This season can't make up its mind,
the trees bald gold red, trees brown and russet
and Indian Red dark as plum pudding, trees
untouched, green as summer's peak...

Now rain through a warm afternoon becomes
snow in the dark, while in the distance fires
boundary the horizon as a tornado tears
the ancient poplar next door from its roots

and storm-driven floods make us still here
homeless. I wake each day to another season.
Our puzzling is the world's. It changes
from a way called 'fixed as the seasons'

to one barely glimpsed through these confusions.
Perhaps one day there will be none, or all
permanently jumbled together— or one nameless
we will wander in wonder— and fear—

strangers on our own ground.

PEACEFALL

No longer do the mountains shout
but let their crimson peaks fade
to twilight's gray: the tremble stops
in bare tree limbs as the wind dies—
even the shutters that drove us mad
with their *flapfapflap* lean against the
house like men after a hard day.

> *I am water: almost all I am is*
> *under the surface. Yet I rise*
> *at her approach, crest on crest,*
> *and pound the shore, long short*
> *short long come to me cometome.*

Never mind my echoes in nature—
I know they rise from confusion and
hunger: what do you expect? I am
only stardust raised to life— of course
my needs struggle for sense!

> *I am a mountain and give an earth*
> *-shaking yawn and stretch as stones*
> *shatter at my feet, ready to chase the sun*
> *until Venus lays a bright finger*
> *across a tremble of darkening waves.*

A mountain is only a slower wave,
and Venus' light touch across the sea
only darkens the night. The greatest
can be least, the softest hard, and I
be more, or less, though I am bound
by the ache in my heart to add myself
to all the other and older already here.

Nightfall and death blur all into one
as deer in the woods sieve
that peace for danger, even as I twist
anxious, in the early a.m., a world
who spins light to dark, death to life.

A strange peace then, yet not even
its trace when I am etched by light again.
Something, I know, eludes me, and
I cannot tell how often I have only slept
and been awakened, or died and been reborn.

ALL WAYS NEW

Winds swirl beneath the gray sky,
cooled by cold waves— a storm long desired
that will not leave but dyes the waves green
that crash on the long shore, and threshes
winter wheat and rye on the mesa where I stand.

This gray, this wind will fill my heart forever.

Come afternoon, the sun sears through
and paints the waves azure, while clouds
are white tongues of flame that lick the hills
which range on range grip the horizon
with their greenly muscled shale.

This white, this blue will fill my heart forever.

WHAT WE CANNOT ESCAPE

When my life makes me a tooth's exposed nerve
    I bawl for a warm embrace to ease the pain
and cure all needs and harms even before
    they are known. Or I sit under a tree like Buddha
until worlds   stars   galaxies   the universe
    tell me pain is the illusion. Or I pen a stoic anthem
like Marcus between days of slaughter to save Rome
    for a worthless son. Yet denial   forbearance
withdrawal   the peace of death   are the illusions.
    Cries of pain pull Buddha from his tree because
he wants wants wants to free us too, while Marcus
    wants us to bear it all with a statue's dignity:
the need to help another defines our hearts.

                    There is no escaping desire.

When we waken to the real the world firms,
    the stars resume their coldhot brilliant paths
through the dark that is bright at the speed of light—
    the paradox our hearts immerse us within—
that lightless bitterness that fuels our hunger to escape,
    that brilliant strength when want is fueled by life's joy
that makes us say despite all we fear, let everything come.

AUTUMN CHOICE

Now just russet oaks and those leaves
    Indian red smolder among the woods'
dwarf pines and bare maples. Of all
    the myriad summer songs just a few notes
make plain the silence. Elsewhere autumn
    feeds into winters' fevers on urban streets:
crowds surge, windows glow with all
    we think we need: all can be bought, and all
seems endlessly reborn.
                      I am torn between
    the hectic surge and the root that hoards
its strength in silence. Tonight as the season's
    first nor-easter prowls around the house
and strips the forest clean and drowns all song
    with its howls, I choose an end to each season:
I don't believe fever on fever equals life.
    A man needs the slow down and ingathering
of his power to defy winter with another spring
    however the years blow past.

MARIGOLDS

Such a yellow burst— late season
   marigolds in their russet vase!
I take them into my soul all week,
   whatever a soul is, even though
their yellow blades must blunt on
   wilting stems.
               Their glow within
is the play of sunlight on water.
   They give the lie to death as
November rains beat the trees
   bare. Their light gives my blood
the smolder of autumn reds
   on such stormy days. It even fills
my dreams with a neon glow.
   If winter makes the days seem less
as well as darker, that inner light
   keeps summer in my step.

REPORT FROM THE FRONT

Everything tumbles together, syringa
    in bloom, sweet clover on the air,
the earth's breath between showers,
    bitterns poised to strike unwary fish
who abandon their granite posts
    with staccato QUAWKQuawkquawks!
when I come too close;
    muskrat who ignores me
as she parts the water with her nose,
    twigs for her den in her teeth;
and hissing snapper with jaws
    even death respects
who slides into tall grass
    that trembles at his passage.
Not far from this suburban edge
    semis from Quebec roll by
with cargoes of furs, blocks of ice,
    cedar sprays, antlers, Eskimo songs
and shrieks of children from farthest north
    where they fence small squares of sky
from wilderness and polar bears. I want
    to link all these in a causal chain,
as though I am he who knows, weighs,
    values, names—
but only this moment by moment teeming
    answers my hunger for sense.

TRANSFORMATIONS

A plain lamppost, lit at twilight,
a plain tree in the rain, yet the
light quicksilvers winter's branches
so some fine mystery, intricate and
natural, transforms our darkness.

A plain sidewalk as I hurry home
shadows doubled by doubled lights:
more double the shadows again
though there are never enough
to shadow all the selves I call my self.

And so, quite simply, to a door
where all in all are known,
and if each moves where any
moment the familiar gives way
to something new, and strange,

and wonderful, it goes so swiftly
we hardly notice the change at all,
however impoverished we would be
if no light shone and no mystery
for a moment transformed our lives.

KALI DANCING BY THE WAVES

There she spins on the sand at the edge
    of the waves' curl and crash, smiling
as she brushes her hair over a shoulder
    and holds her long dress high
as the sea's urgent wash wets her thighs,
    posing as though someone with a camera
snapped, Look! Girl Dancing!
    With each step the world is reborn
and new worlds spin towards infinity
    and love pulses across the universe
beyond measure, this Girl, a girl,
    Unique, commonplace, Woman, a woman.
Her smile is filled with the first light
    that flashed into being when her feet
danced creation, that original light
    we would see if we traveled back in time
banish darkness from the universe.
    I move private moment to moment,
rarely touched by more, Man, a man,
    but with a sudden, certain surprise
feel the glow she lights in my eyes
    echo that beginning that held everything
whose price we go on paying for both
    good and evil, willingly, to be.
Evening falls,
    she smoothes her dress and goes,
but the waves that erase her steps
    I know are echoes, like ourselves,
of that deeper dance by which we move.

ORION IN NOVEMBER

his dog impatient to be off across the sky
    pours the cold north wind through the trees
to make old women creak as it rustles
    their dresses and chills their bones.
And there Stag races up the street towards
    the canyon's refuge in a half-lit lunar light,
hooves clacking on the tarmac as Orion
    leaps to earth in pursuit, club thrown aside,
bow drawn, Sirius' fangs at the Stag's heels.
    Another night as Orion's cold wind shivers
the old women, Coyote lopes by, tongue lolling,
    repeating Stag's flight as the starry duo
leap down again in ground–shaking pursuit.

    Since these I know no guarantee can keep
the stars in place or the night from baring
    something strange: Orion can chase me,
Sirius nip my heels, the hard road batter
    my feet as I race for a secret place
only the hunted heart can find— one where
    Orion leaps past and Sirius loses the scent.
Now when I hear their wild pursuit
    I grip my chair with whitening hands,
my heart loud in the stillness where I hide.

CROWS IN THE PERSIMMON TREE OF PARADISE

Crows caw and dance among the drought
   -singed sun-crisped orange leaves
to tear persimmons with the sun trapped
   in their dangling globes. This, not the apple,
is the tree of paradise— if the sun went nova
   the fruit would be orange balls of fire
within that earth-consuming flame, wings
   darker firetwists as the crows stab and feast:
if goddesses dare me to choose between them,
   I'll give the most human a fruit so ripe
its juice and pulp will burst its thin skin
   and the sun spill out, then dare her to lick
her fingers like a man who can never have
   enough of a good thing.
                    The crows' murder of
wings and black beaks could drive me off,
   but they know death-dealing men too well
and scatter when I clap my hands
   though soon enough they dare return, *though*
soon enough I slide down a shaft of wind
   among them and land where I gulp
gobbets of pulp long past any need, gulp
   so past and present and future hungers
are so sated I become too heavy to fly.
   I hop and caw as though I can tear the sky
to blue shreds with sound, but nothing helps
   until I am in my own skin again on the ground,
and once more with a clap chase the birds
   from my tree,
                   swollen with paradise.

MOUNTAINS, LOGGERHEAD TURTLES, COLD SHOCK ON CAPE COD

A ridge of clouds just clears the bog's
   pines and oaks to the West, as though
a mountain range lost in a blue dream
   free to float where it will. Below them
the fallen sun claws at the remains of the day
   until night folds the frozen clouds
into its basket. This cold is so abrupt
   after the long, warm fall loggerheads
wash up on Bay shores, "Cold Shocked",
   too late to go north around Race Point
then south to safety. I know things are fated,
   but not how, not when: know I cannot trust
all I see   hear   taste   smell   feel
   but have little more to go on. I hold
the dream-mountains lipped in red
   close to heart, and the oaks' russet whispers
after twilight, and the stars who startle
   like clouds of starlings from stripped trees
then cohere, and the waves that pound
   the long Atlantic shore like blind men drums,
and the lights from scattered homes night
   swallows one by one until loneliness alone
remains. Then unseen presences fill the night
   with their hungry 'whos' and howls
and their hearts' heat— that heat
   the frozen loggerheads who now
wash up on Bay shores preserve
   as they slow their heartbeat to one an hour,

adamant to live. Their slow warming fills me
    as we swaddle them to ship south—
they make me realize against what odds,
    we can warm, and live, and love again.

HARE

lopes as only
Hare can, all
fits and starts,
ears sky-sieves
for the whoosh
wings and clenched
claws make
as death stoops
towards him—
but not today,
the sky
bluebare serene
in the heat, the
great Red-tails
who carry death
on their shoulders
perched on a high
leafless limb to
sentinel at noon:
their eyes rake
the cliffsides
for mouseshadow
a mile away.
Nor can Hare
stop his eyes'
search for Coyote's
earth-colored pelt,
or his nose
twitching, tongue
lapping the air
for his rank smell
though the brush

is still.
      He leaps
into sage and
monkey flower
and ceanothus
footed by burning
indian paint-brush:
the path shimmers
with absence— and
something infused
with his life:
imagine
we shy at shadows,
hearts racing, that
our eyes tear
at the light,
or a distant
feathered thunder
teases our ears:
then, perhaps,
we will understand
Hare. He knows
how death's shadow
spreads its wings
within that light
until that light
is gone with a
gut-wrenching
scream and a
blow like a door
with rusted hinges
slammed shut…

THE DEEPWATER ANEMONE IN THE MONTEREY AQUARIUM

Blood-vivid the muscular tube of its body;
    pearlescent arms sieve the water for prey
in depths below the teal and aqueous gleam
    of coral reefs
where the sun, even muted, rolls visibly—

so deep its body is black,
    its arms a slight disturbance in permanent night.
A special display bares its glory
    no one nothing sees where it lives,
that forms no part of its awareness, if aware, there.

Would we appear to other eyes in
    other depths and lights as changed?
Our arms that deal death,
    our careless or brutal or self-absorbed bodies
show as unguessed a beauty?

Are we slides a strange light reveals
    as some scientists claim,
or projections that dance on a black hole's edge,
    afterimages of some swallowed original
that shine above the unfathomable,

lost in our illusion of reality?
    I am haunted by my unknowing.
In my dreamcurrents a red appears
    where there should be darkness alone,
a wavering of arms

at once aglow and invisible
   in depths I should not be able to plumb;
then a flicker of awareness I am dreaming,
   a self-knowledge that is none,
and a bodily sense certain of my weight and years

that is never what it seems, and cannot be what it was.

THE RED-TAILED HAWK OF MY FORGETTING

rises on a thermal of desire over the sunlit seacliff,
  red tail flashing
as he turns head lowered, eyes spears that seek
  the merest telltale motion in the chaparral—
found, he stoops down the angle of his need
  a sharply exhaled breath,
talons hammerheads to the careless head
  whose thin scream they cut off
in a fury of feathers and dust and blood.

Or he perches on eucalyptus trees
winter winds have long stripped,
  that brace one another or they would fall—
Ten years he muses   twenty slides downwind
  in hunger   forty mark him changeless
as I age.
  So I shimmy up the gunbarrel smooth trunk
to meet his gaze, dig my feet in for traction:
  sweat blinds I shake from my eyes until
with a last heave his gaze meets mine.

  'There is the man who day by day
watches me. His father mother children
  are all one, and no one. The years are
long peels of eucalyptus skin that fall
  to the earth, the man always the same
while in me waits one whose greater
  wings one day will spread and shed me
like a husk as he cries into the sun.
  In his gaze I forget my father's name,
mother's, children's, and love forgets mine.
  I am become everyone, and nothing...'

'Here is the hawk who day by day
ignores me. His father mother children
are all one, and no one. The years are
long peels of eucalyptus skin that fall
to the earth, the hawk always the same
while in me waits one who someday
will shed me like a husk as he steps
away from the sun. In his gaze
I forget my father's name, mother's,
children's, and love forgets mine.
I am become everything, and no one...'

Therefore wherever I go I name all I see,
given or new-coined— it is all one to me.
What I record may last while the sun endures,
past that no one can care.
Name by name I chip away at my forgetting.
Each word I give is a name for my love.

LETTER FROM THE LAND OF THE LOTUS EATERS

The clouds are a fogbank whose front of white flame
   marbles with shadows
as it slides north under a sun that enamels the skybowl
   blue.
A day dreams away, and more deeply a night
before the morning wraps us in white mists cold
   as hoarfrost
the noon sun burns off to drive us into shade.

Life here is extremes. The earth shakes
   roads buckle
      homes pulse
         walls fall:
the late hills paint themselves purple, then burn gray
even as winter sprays narcissus' ripe odor in the air
   to war with falling ash.
Birds of paradise blooms snap their wings open
   and spring into flight—
by February camellias daub the air pink and white and a
   blood-dark crimson
until early hot winds tease the plum into bud and bloom
   the next cold wind strips bare.

Now the summer sun blares one note for months
   and daily lips the seaward hills, orange:
again the hot winds blow,
   again autumn purples the hills,
      again fires race relays,
         again death is denied its due
as those fires' deaththroes start seeds that craved their heat...

Children may lie in their blood   and nothing be done:
heads roll or bodies burn   and nothing be done:
we eat from the daily bread of harm we offer one another
    and nothing be done—
but look as my woman and I embrace on the beach
when the orange globe climbs down its ladder of clouds
    and sizzles the sea
how it turns us into silhouettes, icons, postcard perfect dreams
however we yellow and fray.

...Los Angeles, February 2015

FRA JUNIPERO SERRA LINGERS BY HIS CELL AS TOURISTS PASS, LOOKS BACK ON THE RED RIVER OF HISTORY, AND AT LAST CUTS SHORT HIS LINGERING

"Prayerbook, candle, robe, whip—
  you stare at my cell, rich with austerity—
    nothing more marks my passage,
though I furrowed and planted California
  with Missions that bloomed in
    white stucco and brick-red flowers
where before there was nothing.
  I clothed my natives in fields and farms
    in place of the boundary-less sea,
embraced them with settled homes
  in place of their seasonal drift,
    took away their skins and clothed them
so their breasts were no longer
  casually offered to any hand—
    imagine Christ fondling Mary's breasts
like sacks of flour, or squeezing
  her nipples like pebbles.
    I gave them days, weeks, months,
years filled with work
  for timelessness,
    gave them Sundays to pray
Till! Reap! Thresh! On your knees!
  —and if I flogged them for laziness
    I used the whip that beat myself.
Now zealots behead their prisoners
  or hunt them like Yazidis
    to kill to rape to enslave.

Only the slow wear of days
    made mine strangers to themselves.
        I was kind.

I beat my flesh, rip my skin, let my wounds
    rub against my horsehair shirt,
        mixing their blood with mine.

True believers know God loves blood,
    Christ himself joins us
        with the wine of his blood
and flour of his flesh
    in our mouths. Most of all
        He torments innocents to try us.
Our beautiful dreamer, St Francis,
    thought love would make the heart's
        lion lie down like a lamb.
He was so wrong.
    Love is always betrayed,
        betrayal
is our sin and God's threshing wheel.
    Then why do I reach for my whip
        why wonder

Dear God, why did they all die
    in less than a hundred years
        after all those before?
Were You so hungry for their company?
    I beat my flesh, I— ...

        Outside my cell a raven rests
on a cypress branch straight
    as Big Sur cypresses are bent
        by the wind to echo the hills'

steep slopes. He quorks and lifts
    with a ragged flap,
        whether in good omen or bad,
caring about no fate but his own—
    like the birds and the bees
        and the whale who bears the ocean's
weight as he sings downward
    to the dark that holds his prey.
        None of these reaches for more
but holds to himself alone,
    while a man, I tell you, must rise
        to God, through whose flail
we become more than animal.
    Don't think that the sacrifice
        of one man by another
as we strive to reach such perfection
    turns into history's nightmare
        we are forever waking from.
Don't think that each of us should be
    the measure of love, one by one,
        each the summit, each the end
so the red river we feed with our lives
    will clear and run dry.
        No.
That way leaves us bestial as those
    who clash in a blind, resounding dark.

    Do you know I been sainted?
Approved, made someone to pray to
    with a line to God's ear?
        Someone at last beyond doubt?
Let the air empty of summer buzzes
    and clicks and trills.
        Let it empty of children's laughter!

Let the sea grow silent and still.
　　Let no depth nor height shudder
　　　　with the beauty of song.
Let me throw all away to join with You!

　　　I beat my flesh, I—　I beat—　I..."

AFTERWORD

Junipero Serra founded a chain of Franciscan missions in California, and made the Carmel Mission (dedicated 1797) his home. The Indians, taken from their lifestyle that had endured thousands of years, lasted a bare half century more in ill health, drunkenness, and obesity. The last died in Carmel in 1850s. Many of the Missions are still in use, including that at Carmel, where today it is besieged by tourists. Now, Protestant as he was, Bach's music finds a home there each summer in the Bach Festival, while Serra and his faith are reduced to curios and trinkets. Serra has recently been canonized.

St. Francis came to bear Christ's stigmata, but even in his own lifetime lost control of the Franciscan Order he founded to more 'practical' men.

MARIANA

after Millais' *Mariana, 1851*

Blue her dress, blue her mood, blue
    the light that fails towards twilight:
blue, and bored, and pulls her dress
    against her breasts, hands on hips,
head back, half turned to us, eyes closed
    Ahh, she thinks, *how good this feels, if fails*
to meet my hunger for a swollen belly
    to give me a riper shape.
"How long these blue barren days that bind
    my afternoons."

She imagines throwing decorum aside
    to be any man's delight if no one man's,
but that traps her in an image ripeness
    would too much alter.
Or she could wed God and horrify her father
    who turns each suitor away to sell her
to a better, though what long hours a nun
    must fill with prayer   routine   song.
Better to be a new Boadicea
    and burn London again to the ground
in answer to violation, or be Marian and share
    an outlaw love in her own Sherwood.
She pulls her dress tight again   again
    empty
no smile touches her lips.
    If only I could marry, any marriage,
she thinks, then *No one brutal like father*
    using mother like a roast to toss to the dogs

when he's had his fill no, I will give that man
   nothing!
She pities her father.
   Surprised, she takes the thought further—
I pity men, she thinks: I pity their need
   to rush about and lop off each other's parts
to gather power and power and power—
   I pity power.
I pity a man's brief pleasure
   that condemns him to that path
while I grow life from my flesh
   bear life into the world from my flesh,
nurture life with my flesh with such love
   that when my child lies dying in bed or battle-gore
he will not call on comrades or God
   but whisper "Mother"
against the tide of darkness darkening his sight.

She imagines her child feeding from heavy,
   milk-laden breasts,
whether in a great room or hovel
   whatever the violation men inflict;
of joining those women who child by child
   raise each to care, not kill;
of adding hers too to the human stream
   until slowly and invisibly
all men are compelled to love,
   for love alone gives,
   love alone is power,
   love alone is life.
               "But oh," she breathes,
"how long my waiting seems."

RUNES

for Bob Rodman

Night empties a pitcher of rain through my trees.
    Sibelius spins, weeps, rages.
The washer rocks back and forth.

My dog barks, but Orion, behind the blinding storm
    tightens his belt and passes unseen
as my friend cries, grief-stricken, but holds

leechlike to death, sucking life from the dying rune
    of his wife.
I want to say nothing ever dies, but wonder

if I can move so far from despair and fear,
    my own wife so near death once,
my life full of terror from wishing ill,

dreading good, so incomplete a man
    threatened by wholeness or lack in you,
touching the dread of living with my death,

that child who grows in me until one day
    I will be the old skin he sheds.
The truth is very strange, for the best things

are wrung from opposites, closeness
    from hate, courage from despair, life from death:
profoundest love from the grave.

This poem has two true endings. The first (I, as follows) written about 1985 (and published in *Wrestling With The Angel*) is as family mythology then held. After decades of probing that mythology truth requires a different end (II, following), and title... Below are both endings and titles because their shift is emblematic of how truth and history change constantly in our lives.

GRANDFATHER DADDY WILDS, OR: MYTH, MALEVOLENCE, TRUTH

Two images haunt me: Daddy Wilds
willfully slewing his Lincoln around
a hundred miles an hour in the rain,
sure he would spin the right way home:
and, his face battered as a refined
boxer's, shambling from his room
at the end, though warned
any motion would burst his heart.

He was the wild free father brimming
with gifts: cars replacing those
his son smashed, always found unused
in some maiden aunt's garage; money
he went on making as a stockbroker,
after the '29 crash; adoration
of my mother he kept company
as she modelled, outfacing
all the young men until too sick
to face my father down; the castle
and title he spurned because
they weren't good enough:

and he was the man whose mastery
grandmother punished for ten years
with no sex,
who laid in his deathbed while
his son went on smashing things
for someone else to make good, and
his daughter brushed leadpaint and
turpentine around, as if no one was there:
the man who got up and broke
the only heart he knew he could.

I

Some nights I hear him hum
like an engine under the dry
white rain of stars we spin beneath
and I grow dizzy looking for true home
and lie there, short-breathed,
my jaw set like a boxer's against
the pain in my side, weighing
what fuels our pride,
our bribery of love,
our final love of death.

(1985)

or:

II

Or so my father whispered
when I was young. Older,
the truth is precious as breath.
Grandfather smelled no paint
where he lay on the far side
of his home, while all his son smashed
were Germans in North Africa
and France and himself, earning
a Purple Heart: and grandfather
died in bed in my mother's arms,
who was heavy with me—
his death a shockwave in us both.

Some nights I hear him hum
like an engine under the dry
white rain of stars we spin beneath
and I grow dizzy looking for true home
and lie there, short-breathed,
my jaw set like a boxer's against
the pain in my side, weighing
what fuels our pride,
our bribery of love,
our final temptation to love our end—
or if, as he clove to her ripe body
he knew too
life is more pure more adamant
than death.

(2017)

THERE ARE TIMES I DON'T KNOW MYSELF

or where or what the truth is, or the world,
or what is real— and no one comforts me.
Communion, said Luther, is bread and wine

and Christ's body and blood as well,
a mystery to know not understand:
Time, wrote Hawking, ends in black holes
that evaporate so time so life resume

in formulas that do not explain why
there is anything at all: nor is Time,
thought Einstein, the same for me as I recede,
as for you who race towards me— —

   yet my love holds my woman ageless in my arms.

Some days when I break a long walk
by this wall above the shoreward cliff
I see where Los Angeles meets the ocean
through two dead trees by the shore.

Their limbs write nature's mystery in runes
against the blue and teal and steel-hued Pacific
no one can read. Sometimes two red-tails
perch there, always turned seaward

as though to read those words. They at least
are pure desire, true hunger, and the crows
who harry a hawk in midair until he rides
the thermals higher and they scatter.

For hawks the continent behind is bare,
the siren-streamers that arrow to the latest
Seven Eleven murder or the school
where children lie in their blood

are nails scraped across a blackboard
they ignore. So far as they know
no one marches half a world away
to be shot at a border by men

they'd sooner kill, nor do they care
we made the guns, the bullets, the borders,
the hate, the madness, the finger's pressure
on the trigger. There is worse—

when these launch into flight and stoop
to kill with a harsh blow and land on ground
hard as bone from our rainless summer,
the victim silenced mid-cry; or when

the world spirals far below as they tumble
down a shaft of air joined in ecstasy,
they are beautiful, not like us
who do evil and think we do good.

Daily I look for them, here even absent
as now squirrel, now hare, sieve the light
for their shadows and crows guard their nests
as God's creation grows at speeds

we measure but don't know towards that day
its wave will run up a distant, darkened shore,
its starry foam thin, and at last disappear.
Why then write in my diary

in the red ink we use for our histories
the night 's rise or the stars' demise
in the obliterate sun, or care if I have
the strength to bear my freedom

and define whether I too will destroy,
or fill the air with bliss; or wonder
if the runes scratched by these trees
on the teal and blue and steel-hued sea

translate to *why why   why*; or why
the answer that moves through my guilt
and innocence as light through glass
is *love love   love*;

   for while I love my woman is ageless in my arms

and her beauty grows past the familiar years
to something new unknown, the mystery
that keeps my heart in this world, the root
that let me grow to the man I am.

HAUNTINGS IN WESTON

Fifty years— the number alone amazes—
since I lived here, the home of all
the 'where and whens?' of my youth.
Memory embraces where I left off, as though
the life lived fully elsewhere is a dream.
But those once so close are old, or gone,
the girls gone into their children's lives—
and then I was young and full of anger.

I wonder if a Cro Magnon savage
wandering from cave to cave found one
hole or another, or his wandering, *home*—
if he puzzled whether to stay each time
he stood again where once he was young
though those once so close are old, or gone,
the girls gone into their children's lives—
and then he was young and full of anger.

I am drawn to visit this place, and these
granite cliffs where I found solace
from my family's argument-riven home,
puzzled whether to stay though those
once so close are old or gone,
the girls into their children's children—
and then I was young and full of anger.
I come home only to leave again and again.

SO, LEOPARDI

...for Jeanne

        ill and ever more deformed,
you say how the most beautiful woman turns
into bones tainted with mud, and that you want
death to relieve your suffering, all the harder
because no one requites your love.
                             Imagine
you marry a dreamgirl straight from Hollywood,
drink down her embraces like a relapsed alcoholic;
father children, or simply, live longer in less pain—
then would you still say
                        Tanto alle morta inclina
                        D'amor la disciplina
love's law bends us all towards death?
Day, you say acutely, follows night   but youth
and beauty aren't repeated by nature.
        Ma la vita mortal, poi che le bella
        Giovinezza spari, non si colora
        D'altra luce giammai, ne d'altra aurora.

I have known passion when my woman stole
backstairs to my rented room those years ago
when we lived apart. Her clothes fell like water
shaken from her hair walking from the waves
as I pulled her to me and imagined something infinite
beyond the rattling bedframe and our moans
as ecstasy released us from mind and marrow —
        E il naufragar m'e dolce in questo mare—
there is a sweet foundering, there a sweet sea.

Now when light seeps then streams through
our morning window it shows her wrinkled face
through which I see her loveliness too.
You couldn't learn, dead at 39, how all times
entwine with each other so that each day
contains all the days that came before, and makes
something far beyond your sad, sonorous, Italian
music, something new, something far richer.

Drawn from "Canti XXVII, XXXIII" and "XII" in that order,
after Jonathan Galassi's translations in the Penguin *Giacomo
Leopardi: Canti*.

ANSWER TO RUMI

*Natural beauty is a tree limb reflected
in the water of a creek, quivering there, not
there....*

*The whole of the world is a form for truth...*Rumi

Beloved... All week storms teased with no more
    than a moment's spatter in the heat,
once lightning so distant thunder rolled in silence.
    Now a waterfall of rain sluices down the steep sky
through the shore-lined iron trees and higher palms
    under the star and moonless sky,
though those gleam unbroken above our airs.
    With tropic swiftness the storm is done,
only the waveroll at the cliff's foot carries to us here
    from the rock-ledged shore. The touch of cool,
cleansed tradewinds on our linked flesh, our unseen
    sheen of sweat, relieves and soothes...
All this is equally real, the love I feel for you, you,
    your glance darker than the dark room, flesh and bone
down to our star-made atoms that hold within
    the forces that forge the universe,
those strings of power that ring in our atoms' voids,
    so that at root everything is music.
God is stone, and blood, and hurt, or cry, or joy, or nothing.
    Yet of these, simple, complex, real—
heaven   hell   past   future   it is passion's evanescence
    our sweat and breath and embracing air
and the night's warm arms—
    our fulfilled or broken hearts—
age in youth who finds youth in age—
    that are all we have to be who we are, life and life's purpose

however we strain to say the unsayable.
 Hold to me sweetheart, the night is still ours to explore,
whether in spring or fall, we two who are one but two:
 You and I are the end.
  You and I are the beginning.

Kauai, 2018

MARS DESCENDS

Mars hangs below the moon
    over the ocean's western edge,
a red ribbon over the waves after
    the violet orange-scented twilight fades.
Once we imagined cities there
    with strange and familiar people,
some four-armed who rode beasts
    like dinosaurs, some tall and spindly
who swayed like reeds in a wind,
    some ourselves able to leap into flight
and wield a hero's strength.
    Or we thought a god sulked there
from his anger at a goddess
    faithful only to love. Now
we know not to fill Mars' deserts
    with dreams and nightmares.
Mystery recedes...
                Even our deeps
    yield their crushed secrets.
I am reduced to myself,
    monstrous, fragile, heroic, broken
but for one I slide beside each night
    who in a mystery that endures
makes from even my violence
    through the steadiness of her heart
what the goddess could not,
    a man who can be loved.

THE ORWELL AT TWILIGHT MIRRORS THE

slowshift clouds as the wind curls
on itself and yawns asleep. No
ocean-going hulls cleave the channel
nor does a tidal ebb or flow
stir the water. The Ipswich freighters
are snugged quayside, the great red-sailed
barges, and sloops and cutters, lie moored

outside the buoyed way, sails furled...
I wonder in this repose, as if before
a statue or a motionless mobile,
what have we put of ourselves
into metal and stone, wood, line
or sail, risked in the winds
or carelessly at the helm because

we are always at risk and
put ourselves into the world in
some incomplete way, as though
to know ourselves by parts. Earlier
Fanny needed two hands on her rudder
to plow a straight furrow for
our wake, gentler when the gusts
eased and I could drive one-handed:

and longed as quickly again
for the wind to heel us over,
for water to foam over *Fanny's*
bow and sheer joy drive us through
roughening swells towards a horizon
cloaked in spray and cloud and promise
if I could just go far enough long enough—

and did neither, not because the land
is better or my hunger for the infinite less,
but because my woman called me
back from that wild beauty
to something more modest and defined
yet richer, because her embrace makes me
whole. Even now her love calls
me from this perfect repose, home.

...The River Orwell bounds one side of the Shotley Peninsula in East Anglia.

QUANTUM DREAMS AND THE PHYSICS OF LOVE

We know so little of our minds' physics,
   not even if our linear, daylit logic
is more or less true than our dreamsleep's
   where near and far then and now
lie entwined as lovers, two bodies, one,
   two minds in ecstasy, none.
We say Newtonian cause and effect
   is truer than quantum mysteries
where realities divide from each other
   yet share at once each other's fate,
the improbability we scout in our dreams.
   We wake for one, sleep for the other,
to be more than incomplete. Tell me
   the heart is muscles and chambers
and bloodflow: not love's metaphor
   but tissue and pulse,
that metaphor is poetry, and poetry
   is not real; tell me all
that makes life desirable roots
   in a forward driving time although
our minds are no steadier than scraps
   of paper blown down city streets.
But then why, eyes open, do I see
   my woman's lines relax as she sleeps
beside me now even as she now creeps
   upstairs to my room overlooking
Commonwealth Avenue so long ago,
   where soon we cannot tell ourselves apart?
Yes, I know. Who lives in such simultaneities
   and stays sane? erases the straight line

between then, there; here— now;
    young, then; now— old?
and does not go mad?
    And yet tell me this old woman fails
to hold me then, that young woman
    fails to wrap me in her arms now!
For love's reality is stranger even
    than those quanta bound together
however the void between them grows—
    I know you cannot lie here now, relaxed
unless you lie there then in passion
    all ages embraced at once in one's embrace.

THIS IS ALL

My heart is my body's poem
my mind a simile of light
though insight is a meteor
that flashes across the bone vault
and leaves what follows darker.
At times I feel all I am is
a metaphor for something else.
Sometimes in another's arms
I am all forgetting: sometimes
I am caught in the hollow drum
of my want or am invaded by
a child's tears or laughter; or
anger sweeps me away or
music makes me soar or
silence fills with my echo,
for my heart with all
its regular meter plays
a variable song. My road
is straight, it divides, tangles,
goes up goes down and
sometimes dreamlike loops
overhead on itself. I live
in this mystery of unknowing
where I can never say 'this is me,
this is it, this is all, I have arrived.'

THE ORANGES OF GUIMARAES

for Martin Bax

fall in circles around their trees—
  within the shade their globes
turn green with mold: outside,
  the sun slowly changes them
to brown husks. At night they
  astonish, for their yellow coals
glow long after the sun goes down.

  Now there are no monks
to harvest them, or to clear
  the ground, prune old branches
or hollow the surrounding earth
  into wells to fill with water.
Just the wind hurries through
  the scarlet oaks, eucalyptus taller
than the redwood planted among
  these strangers; hurries through
the tulip tree's chalice of limbs
  above the holly's sharp leaves
where the berries on rare, gray days
  glow like dwarf stars.

Nor does it matter
they are abandoned. Fruit must fail
   and limbs die too fast to be pruned,
as the avocado died in my yard
   an ocean and continent away—
some things are indifferent
   to where or who we are, whether
an orange or a man, whose flesh
   no more stays firm than these
whose juicy pulp shrivels
   in their rind:

                    nor does it matter
these oranges write no poems
   to celebrate or lament their lives
unlike myself who spills words
   on the wind. Yet I lie down
among their spray of small suns
   because I want to steal their power
to go on lighting the dark
   long after they have fallen.

THE
AMERICAN
VOICE

its nature, form, and bearing

We have been misguided in America for a long time about the real nature of the American Voice, a misunderstanding abetted by the unfortunate connection of American poets and poetry with the American university where one false vision after another sweeps over the country with each critical craze. We can sweep away this nonsense if we look at three iconic poets in their own time, Walt Whitman, Robinson Jeffers, and Robert Lowell. A recognizable pattern of development and outlook emerges from their consideration, which is the essence of our poetic voice and explains Whitman, Jeffers, and Lowell's stature at their apogees.

All three undergo a *quantum leap* in ability or direction which little foreshadows. This is combined with the *rapture* of visionary insight, a subsequent assumption of a *common stance* with mankind, and a *move to clarity* in their poetic language. They adopt an *epic breadth*, and make the claim they know the way to *health*. Variously they *turn to nature* and/or *confront the real form and pressure of America*. All go through a period of confusion and loss of direction as the consequence of an *inflation* growing out of their earlier work. All surprisingly regain their voice and power in a late *return*.

Whether this is a uniquely American and poetic pattern is open to question; Whitman spoke of Americans of all times and places... A woman poet would bring other issues to the table, to say nothing of those poets confronting the ethnic prejudices rampant in this country. These features are not a schema, and they are realized by each of these iconic poets in strikingly different ways, although there are surprising overlaps in their visions and diagnoses of *our* present condition despite their differences. These traits of the American Voice are coeval in these three iconic poets with the nature of the task they undertake, whether to celebrate, destroy, or renovate.

1. Quantum Leap

Whitman produced nothing noteworthy before the publication of the first edition of *Leaves of Grass* in 1855. Before this he served an undistinguished apprenticeship in printing, functioned as a schoolteacher, and went into journalism. An idiot brother often shared his bed. After being fired in 1848 from the *Brooklyn Eagle* he traveled to New Orleans for two months and on his return was a changed man. No one is sure if the journey brought out his homosexuality, or whether that remained latent. But on his return Whitman gave up his previous dandyism, transformed his appearance into a rough common man's— and wrote almost all the poems for the first edition of *Leaves of Grass*. That work starts with these lines from "Song of Myself" declaring universal brotherhood and identity,

> I celebrate myself,
> And what I am I assume you shall assume,
> For every atom belonging to me as good as
>   belongs to you.

Few took notice, but Emerson was among those and wrote a famous letter saluting Whitman as a prodigy. The letter created a sensation when, to Emerson's surprise, Whitman swiftly had it published. *Leaves of Grass* with that letter now created a larger sensation. Yet few agreed with Emerson initially in America: Whitman spent his lifetime demanding the respect he thought due him from his native country, however celebrated abroad he became.

Leaves of Grass altered perceptions about poetry and America. Whitman invented the persona of the proletarian, democratic bard whose song of himself stood for the song of every man. He sloughed off the poetic tradition and in cadenced, rhythmic free verse influenced by his love for operatic aria celebrated himself and the world around him with an unprecedented frankness and boldness. When an American poet looks back over the American past for a founding voice, Whitman stands at the door.

The quantum leap for Robinson Jeffers was as remarkable. Thirty-eight years of little achievement preceded *Tamar* in 1924, and *Roan Stallion, Tamar, and Other Poems* in 1925. The impact of those books, unlike *Leaves of Grass*, was immediate. Jeffers towered over the 1920s and 30s and, though declining, the 1940s. We have lost the sense of his size, but then he easily matched if not exceeded Pound and Eliot in the public eye. While they left the country, he remained, casting his shadow over his contemporaries.

When his break-through came he asserted a oneness with Nature, drawing his poetic strength from a universal source.

> Mother, though my song's measure is like your
>   surf-beat's ancient rhythm I never learned
>   it of you.
> Before there was any water there were tides of
>   fire, both our tones flow from the older
>   fountain.
>   from "Continent's End"

This grave tone and tidal line are decidedly Jeffers. The direct address, with its assumption of a unity between you and me, and an overt claim of man's unity with nature, is as marked as in Whitman's "For every atom belonging to me as good as belongs to you." Again the quantum leap from the uninspired earlier work lands Jeffers in a shaped but clearly free verse rhythm of his own creation that subsumed traditional poetic elements, like Whitman.

Unlike Whitman and Jeffers, Robert Lowell enters publication admired and rewarded, a scion of a bloodline including James Russell Lowell, Amy Lowell, and Boston

Brahmins. He was an approved follower of the ideas of the New Critics who spurned Robinson Jeffers. Both *Lord Weary's Castle* in 1946 (Pulitzer Prize) and *The Mills of the Kavanaughs* in 1951 preceded his quantum leap. Their poetry is that of a specialist, traditional in usages, while Lowell's personal 'I' is almost lost in his effects.

In 1959 Lowell broke through this preciousness in *Life Studies* which had an immediate, galvanic impact on poetic practice and Lowell's reputation, uncorking 40 years and more of confessional poetry and reaching past academic, specialist confines towards the common American man and woman. Here is the start of "My Last Afternoon with Uncle Devereux Winslow".

I.

"I won't go with you. I want to stay with
    Grandpa!"
That's how I threw cold water
on my Mother and Father's
watery martini pipe dreams at Sunday
    dinner.
…Fontainebleau, Mattapoisett, Puget Sound….
Nowhere was anywhere after a summer
at my Grandfather's farm.

Lowell's previous formalism is set aside for the cadences of prose and speech, rhyme apparently accidental. Tradition is subsumed within a Whitmanesque and Jeffersian speaking out to a man not assumed to be a fellow poet but a fellow American. It is *that American's* contemporary language turned into poetry, a profound divide from Lowell's earlier usage and another *quantum leap*. Lowell himself was proudest of the Part Four sequences concluding *Life Studies*: he knew he had broken out from strait-jacket modernism. In so doing he transcended also his merely Boston, Brahmin roots and spoke to the nation.

2. Rapture

Visionary experience or *transcendence* or *mystical experience* or, as we would say in our bitterer age, *madness* or *mania*, might do as well as *rapture* here. These defining figures were transformed in life and poetry by visionary experience whose end impact is some form of rapture. The *rapture* is quite straightforward with Whitman. He writes in '5', "Song of Myself":

> Swiftly arose and spread around me the peace
>   and joy and knowledge that pass all the art
>   and argument of the earth;
> And I know that the hand of God is the
>   elderhand of my own,
> And I know that the spirit of God is the eldest
>   brother of my own,
> And that all the men ever born are also my
>   brothers…and the women my sisters and
>   lovers.

We are faced with one of the most surprising facets of the iconic, defining American poet: *he* and *his poetry are shaped by a 'mystical' experience out of which flows not a renunciation but an engagement with the world*, an experience in which *all* is seen to cohere.

I imagine many reacting negatively to the idea 'we are all Americans' implied in Whitman's idea the American is "fittest for his day", and in the phrase "Americans of all nations at any time" in his Preface to *Leaves of Grass*. But what is meant here is an ideal of human brotherhood to be attained through a vision of a compassionate, moral, transported yet immediate identification of one man with All— all men, all nature.

Jeffers presents an equally clear case of the impact and *rapture* of vision transforming his plebian life and work. We are no more sure than we are with Whitman at what precise hour it struck, or if it was a series of insights that cumulatively transfigured Jeffers instead of one sudden blaze. These things are not susceptible to critical reduction and explanation. We see them through their impact in work published after their arrival, work impossible without such transport.

The key elements of Jeffers' vision are the violence at the center of Nature and the sickness in our hearts, combined with the belief that if only we look outward from our obsessive self-regard to the enormous beauty of being, the handiwork of God, we will see the wholeness of existence and find peace. He holds to that even though Jeffers' God is anything but tame.

Whitman knew metaphorically and Jeffers factually three quarters of a century later that the atoms we are made of were forged in the stars. We are one with nature and its processes, for Jeffers: if we could hold to that perspective then even the most horrible of our inhumanities "…would be found/ Clean as a child's or like some girl's breathing who dances/ alone/By the ocean-shore, dreaming of lovers" (from "Natural Music"). His most famous rapturous lines come from "Roan Stallion" in the sequence starting,

                                        Humanity is
        the start of the race; I say
Humanity is the mould to break away from,
        the crust to break through, the coal to kindle
        into fire
The atom to split.

We are within the Emersonian sense of a transcendent reality under or overlying the delusions of immediate experience, and again a poet comes to that understanding in his own way through visionary experience that leads to an outburst of genius. Jeffers wrote hundreds of lyric poems from 1919-1938, 18 long narratives, often epic in length, and four verse dramas.

Robert Lowell is no less part of this tradition of *rapture* though he typically inverts the large Whitmanesque or Jeffersian gesture, distancing and diminishing his experience with denial and irony, although irony is always a diminuendo of greatness if the dominant tone, as in our own era. He also swiftly fled the astonishing arc of *Life Studies*, 1959, *Imitations*, 1961, and *For The Union Dead*, 1964.

Yet there is a double irony here, for Lowell can be seen somewhat mischievously as the quintessential *romantic* poet with his mixture of sanity and insanity. He was bipolar, an extreme manic-depressive in our more knowledgeable and darker language. The aura of mystery and genius madness was once thought to offer is to us a worn and dangerous idea. We reach for a pill or end in an asylum if need be, as indeed Lowell did in 1949, 1954, and 1957-1958, to mention only the main occasions. Lowell himself would have given the 'romantic' idea no credence: insanity was not a literary flourish for him, while the astringent, sterile prescriptions of the New Critics before he broke away with *Life Studies* took a dim view of personal, emotional expressiveness, let alone poetic directness.

Lowell's madness made him fear *the excitement of poetry itself*. Part of the treatment of his breakdowns in the later 1950s as *Life Studies* gestated was a requirement he write only *prose*. As Frank Bidart writes in his Introduction to Lowell's *Collected Poems*, "The thrill associated with madness, unreachable when sane, is the sensation all "coheres."' The coherence of personal identity and the wider life of man, world, and/or God at the heart of Whitman and Jeffers' transforming, visionary rapture is *insanity* for Lowell.

Yet not least ironic is Lowell's paradoxical *appeal to coherence* built into the break-through poems of *Life Studies* and *For The Union Dead*.

My whole eye was sunset red,
the old cut cornea throbbed,

I saw things darkly,
as through an unwashed goldfish globe.
Nothing! No oil for the eye, nothing to pour
on those waters or flames.
I am tired. Everyone's tired of my turmoil.
 from "Eye and Tooth", *For The Union Dead*

He assumes across the gulf separating ego from ego
I will consider myself a brother in pain, that he and I have a
community of interests, that our points of contact are so strong
and so familiar he can speak to me in this seemingly unpoetic
language. This is Whitman and Jeffers' assumption, but Lowell
is the spokesman for entropy, the inability of experience to
cohere, of things flying apart, even as he makes the underlying
assumption that that is our common lot about which he can
speak coherently, to "Everyone".

Yet...

There is one direction where Lowell did make the
large, *overtly* inclusive leap and claim of the defining poet.
His *Imitations* seizes the representative figures in the poetic
tradition stretching back to Homer and transforms them into
Americans. "I have tried to write alive English and to do what
my authors might have done if they were writing their poems
now and in America", he claims in his Introduction. "Most
poetic translations come to grief and are less enjoyable than
modest photographic prose translations," he adds. Therefore...
His first two Sappho poems actually are "new" poems, Villon
is "stripped", Hugo's "Gautier" is halved, and so on. He adds
stanzas to poems by the perfectionist Rilke. "I have dropped
lines, moved lines, moved stanzas, changed images and altered
meter and intent." It is breath-taking as a conceit, and the most
brilliant book of its kind we are likely to see, and embodies
Whitman's view that, "The Americans of all nations at any time
upon the earth have probably the fullest poetical nature." In

Lowell the Americanization of the European tradition reaches a climax.

However these iconic poets are compromised, however at moments they may feel "frizzled, stale and small" (Lowell, "Home After Three Months Away"), their poetic voice is larger than life, no matter what damage they suffer from the vagaries of undisputed disease, despair, or debilitating irony.

But Lowell's provincialism needs remarking. Like a good East Coast American poet, Lowell scion and Bostonian, he looks constantly back to Europe with one eye, while the other stares inward examining his sanity and motivation as obsessively as John Adams two hundred years ago. There are no Asian poets in *Imitations*, no Spanish or Latin American, no African, not even poets working in the English tradition who require translation: Anglo Saxon, Middle English, Chaucer. The narrowness of view is a cultural debilitation, a rut so deep Lowell couldn't see it. Worse, it is an academic debilitation, brilliant, shining, giving us a great book and a great creative moment, but one for other poets and academics, not one that reaches out to the common man on the street. It is a bright flash in a small room high in an ivory tower.

3. Common Stance, and: 4. Move to Clarity

Both these elements are integral to the quantum leap as well as the rapture of visionary insight underlying these poets. Their rapture, insight, vision, metaphysical transport, what you will, gives them a radical urge to put themselves forward and to be understood by all.

> In all people I see myself, none more and not
>   one a barleycorn less,
> And the good and the bad I say of myself I say
>   of them.
>   from "Song of Myself"

Great, humane men have made claims akin to this in the past: Terrence wrote "humani nil a me alienum oputo"—'nothing human is alien to me'— while Montaigne asserted he was his own best study for understanding mankind. But they spoke with restraint of themselves while the American defining poet extravagantly makes the claim to universality overtly, at length, clearly, and directly.

Directness is a hallmark of Jeffers, too.

> The old woman sits on a bench before the door
>   and quarrels
> With her meager pale demoralized daughter.
> …
> I see that once in her spring she lived in the
>   streaming arteries,
> The stir of the world, the music of the
>   mountain.
>
>   from "Fawn's Foster Mother", *Cawdor*

He wants us to feel the old woman's decline, to understand what is now lost from the time of "her spring". It is because the old woman once lived "in the streaming arteries" that she quarrels with her daughter, whose failure stems from not living in "the music of the mountain", at one with nature. She is too limited, consequently, and her failure is one of vision as well as nerve, a moral "demoralized" fault. Jeffers is not concerned to be precious, experimental, surreal, traditionally rhyming or metered, minimal, maximal, or any other such thing but, like Whitman, wants us to 'get it'. The more style matters, the less a poet has to say and the more, ultimately, the style will render him hermetic to future readers.

The same urgency to be understood underlies Lowell's work in *Life Studies*. Now he has something to say that's too important for his former word games or critical proprieties. He too was prepared to and did break with just those things in his quantum leap. The move to a common stance and move to clarity go hand in hand with an act of defiance to the received wisdom of traditional and prevailing poetic practice, and leads to the development of such a poet's own way of speaking the common language of the day with fresh power. In fact Lowell's abandonment of poetry as he recovered from his hospitalization in the late 1950s for prose helped him move in the direction of his breakthrough poems. In "Father's Bedroom" he starts off with a list, moving from thin blue threads on the bedspread, blue-dotted curtains, a sandpapered broad-planked floor, and Vol. Two of a book by Lafcadio Hearn.

> Its warped olive cover
> was punished like a rhinoceros hide.
> In the flyleaf:
> "Robbie from Mother."

The poem ends,

> This book has had hard usage
> on the Yangtze River, China.
> It was left under an open
> porthole in a storm.
>   from *Life Studies*

He could be talking to any contemporary American. There is no rhyme, no set meter. The only obviously poetic usage is "punished like a rhinoceros hide", and that seems merely colorful in context, and implies a degree of usage that is affecting. Jeffers writes of what would characterize the true poet:

> ...I believe that our man would turn away from
> the self-conscious and naïve learnedness, the
> undergraduate, unnatural metaphors, hiatuses,

361

labored obscurity, that are too prevalent in contemporary verse. His poetry would be natural and direct. He would have something new and important to say, and just for that reason he would wish to say it clearly. He would be seeking to express the spirit of his time (as well as all times)....

from "Poetry, Gongorism, And
A Thousand Years"

It is these poets' underlying vision that sparks their transformation of prosody, not accumulating practice. Lowell would not have reached *Life Studies* without his rapture, or Whitman written at all. Equally decisive is the poet's explanation of his stance and prosody. Jeffers we saw ascribed his lines to the long beat of Pacific surf, so unlike the nervous Atlantic's, and the way the Pacific's surf and tides echo the earlier cosmic tides of fire.

These poets' efforts to speak of by and for every man, to give our daily lives an aesthetic shape, may involve illusion and be a form of folly, but it is a noble folly, and necessary. To shape our consciousness into a creative self-awareness through their own, to give size and meaning to the common life of industrial, post-industrial, and technological man may involve illusion and be a form of folly, but it is a noble folly, and necessary. Illusion can be the road to madness, but in the hand of the poetic personality of one of these defining poets illusion can be instead the road to meaning and, yes, redemption, however fleetingly bound to the experience of a particular poem.

It is in this sense the "American" effort may be the "human" effort to civilize, to humanize the unprecedented, continuous, revolutionary changes through which global society is moving with such frequent disruption and dismay.

5. The Epic Stance

"Song of Myself" is an epic of a transported self doing his utmost to communicate his vision to the wider world: Whitman's ambition for *Leaves of Grass* is biblical in sweep. Epic is similarly inseparable from Jeffers, whether in the epics beginning with *Tamar* or in his stance of godlike clarity and perspective through which he communicates his vision of health. Lowell is the least epic of the three, although that crucial element is there, not in the longer poems preceding *Life Studies*, but in his own extended, interrupted 'song of myself' starting with Part IV of *Life Studies*, continuing through 1964's *For The Union Dead*, mislaid in the various *Notebooks* and the derivative works following, and resumed near the end of his life in *Day by Day*. Like Whitman his epic is himself, albeit expanded to recover the nuclear family from fiction and drama for poetry. In this respect Jeffers stands apart in the long poems, speaking through personae. Later he admits

> Thinking of the narrative poems I made, which
>   always
> Ended in blood and pain, though beautiful
> enough— my pain, my blood....
>   from "But I Am Growing Old and
>   Indolent", *The Beginning and the End*

In the end there is only ourself to offer to another.

6. Health and the lyric 'I'

One of the primary claims of the break-through these poets make is that they have found the way to health for all, a claim made directly in Whitman and Jeffers, ironically as usual by Lowell.

Central to this assertion, and clear from the common

stance and move to clarity, is the reinvention of the lyric 'I'. I cannot stress too strongly that these poets make a claim for authenticity, that their 'I' speaks themselves and that our 'I' is included in their own. This claim is at the heart of their poetic 'stance', of their voice. Nothing is as easy to misunderstand as this lyric 'I'. In the confessional poetry sparked by Lowell the lyric 'I' becomes revelatory in a merely personal way that reduces us to voyeurs. That is not the lyric 'I' at all, just someone's 'me.' The lyric 'I' is at once personal and impersonal or multipersonal, the 'I' that Whitman and Jeffers speak when they refer to the multitudes they contain in themselves, namely, of us.

Lowell's claim is clear in the autobiographical poems of *Life Studies*: 'here I stand, here is my authentic experience of self and family'. Authenticity is as troubled a concept as the lyric 'I' with which it is profoundly entwined. It is easily confused with confessional sincerity. But the nature of authenticity goes beyond the sincere. A sincere person may reveal something about himself we accept as true of him, but the authentic person simultaneously lays bare and claims a reality abidingly truthful about himself *and us*. That is the steel in the lyric 'I', and why it is so much more than simply a 'sincere me'.

By contrast the inauthentic is a matter of coterie and clique, passing fad, social or personal dementia.

So Lowell's claim that universal coherence is madness leaves him as we saw only the immediate, individual and fragmented, his Mother, Father, Grandfather, Grandmother, and his own incoherent, recurrently bi-polar self. This is the way it is he says, this is reality, and because his description is so apt for the second half of the 20th Century he paradoxically speaks for us, too. "We are being proven in a sort of secular purgatory: there is no earthly paradise on the horizon," he writes, far from Whitman's optimism and oddly close to Jeffers' intense criticism of contemporary life. Equally revealing is his use of "we". All of us, not just Lowell, are going through this purgatory. By focusing on and asserting the authenticity of these immediacies, Lowell implies if each of us does the same then we too will live in reality and sanity, however we may be denied larger consolations.

To share Lowell's lyric 'I' is to experience the only coherence available, that of personal integrity and fidelity to the unvarnished reality of an endlessly purgatorial world.

That is why these poets are all religions unto themselves. They cannot have any other worldview to communicate their quantum leap and rapture, they cannot be a figure like Eliot, slipping into the reassurances of a received faith. It is just those faiths which poets like these *come to replace* because traditional faiths have lost their ability to express our experience to to offer the health and balance we crave. Equally, these poets cannot find a selfish salvation. They are on the cutting edge of the time each in his own day thought "modern", and what they express is for us all.

Jeffers asserts an authentic, healthy self communicated by the lyric 'I' without Lowell's irony. The *health* these poets claim is a state of mind as well as way of living created in the moment(s) of their *quantum leaps* and *raptures*. The lyric 'I' of *that* Jeffers or Whitman or Lowell *is* indeed, entirely well. *The American lyric 'I' is a visionary reinvention of the healthy self for the common man*, or in our so much less interesting language, the general audience or reader or public...

The Jeffersian road to health is to turn outward from our incestuous self absorption, as in "Humanity is/the start of the race" from the sequence quoted earlier from "Roan Stallion". He wants to be remembered

> Entire and balanced when I was younger,
> And could lift stones, and comprehend in the
>   praises the cruelties of life.
>   from "Ante Mortem", *An American*
>   *Miscellany*

because "The beauty of things was born before eyes and sufficient to/itself" (from "Credo"), and "our world is not/ perfectly separate from nature's, private and mad" ("Calm and Full the Ocean", *The Double Axe*).

Turn to nature, live in nature, work stone, live within the seasons, within natural rhythms: see things *sub species aeternitas*, and health awaits us to the extent possible in our fallen world, especially in the world of 1914-1945. In that way we are "entire and balanced" and understand the "praises and cruelties of life" in which all is "equally beautiful".

Whitman has the great benefit of coming first and from a time we in a careless moment almost think innocent, publishing *Leaves of Grass* five years before the Civil War which transformed his time to one of still unparalleled national suffering. Assertions of health seem to leap off nearly every page of "Song of Myself", including the famous "Who goes there! hankering, gross, mystical, nude?/...And I know I am deathless/...My foothold is tenoned and mortised in granite,/I laugh at what you call dissolution,/And know the amplitude of time" (from lines 388-421).

This unabashed statement of multitude, size, and health would be impossible to accept if not so obviously metaphorical an assertion of the wellness and fullness flowing from an acceptance of common, universal selfhood. *Come join me, loaf, observe, celebrate our common humanity, our common selfhood flowing from the Universal Self* Whitman says in effect, and be "sound", "entire and balanced" (Jeffers), or be the reader who "was to believe he was getting the *real* Robert Lowell" as Lowell said trying to explain the desired impact of his 'autobiographical' poems, meaning, of course, "getting" *his* reality and troubled sanity.

I repeat here that these elements are not part of some critical schema. They do not exist as separate experiences. The *common stance, move to clarity, quantum leap*, and *rapture* are different facets of a unitary experience that can only be communicated through the *lyric* 'I' as these poets assert the claim to *health*. Analysis breaks these elements apart for the sake of discussion, but their experience is one of constant unification for poet and reader, and it is the *experience* that is all-important. These poets are, ultimately, inescapable because they write of permanent things within the upheavals of our present experience and recall us to the enduring in ourselves.

7. Turn to Nature, and/or: 8. Confronting the Real Form and Pressure of America

Part of the *quantum leap* and underlying vision behind these poets' *rapture* is a confrontation with our industrial, post-industrial, and technological societies.

In "The Purse Seine" Jeffers first evokes sardine fishermen working at night drawing in their nets, the phosphorescent shoals of fish beating the water to a frenzied brilliance as the nets tighten, sea lions watching, "sighing in the dark". Then he evokes how brilliant a city at night seems, just like the seine net gathering luminous fish in the dark. He thinks

> ... We have geared the machines and locked all
>   together into interdependence; we have
>   built the great cities; now
> There is no escape. We have gathered vast
>   populations incapable of free survival,
>   insulated
> From the strong earth, each person in himself
>   helpless, on all dependent. The circle is
>   closed, and the net
> Is being hauled in. They hardly feel the cords
>   drawing, yet they shine already. The
>   inevitable mass disasters....

This is a chilling vision of our history and our technological changes as special cases of blind natural process inexorably working its way to a disastrous end while we shine brightly within a net we hardly know is there.

There are now computer 'apps' that allow a view of the world that is bright in the daylight zone, and marked by brilliant webs of light in the night zone. It's hard not to think of Jeffers' prophetic poem then as we sink further into the upheavals of climate change, violence, and pandemic.

Now we can understand the grandeur and tragedy of Robert Lowell. From a Jeffersian point-of-view Lowell is down there in the city as the nets tighten. In "Home After Three Months Away" Lowell evokes his return from the hospital and mental illness, and ends, "I keep no rank or station./Cured, I am frizzled, stale and small" (*Life Studies*). This is not just open, not just brave, but heroic: *that we should care, with the nets closing*— without a question mark or, for once, an ironic, defensive twist. This personal, unsparing bitterness continues in "For The Union Dead" as Lowell meditates on Colonel Shaw and his heroic, doomed Black regiment in the Civil War, sparked by considering urban redevelopment which has destroyed the old Aquarium of his childhood in another part of town. The last stanza goes

> The Aquarium is gone. Everywhere,
> giant finned cars nose forward like fish;
> a savage servility
> slides by on grease.

In this depraved scene even Hiroshima is commercialized. There is, too, a fusion of natural and urban as "giant finned cars nose forward like fish", a hint of the natural process in which we are caught that is so marked in Jeffers.

Whitman saw the poet as spanning the continent, one who "reflects what is inbetween ". He saw the future and asserted *Leaves of Grass* was written for the American far West, imagining "a free original life there", American civilization grasping the continent and finding on the West Coast "a newer, mightier world" ("Pioneers! O Pioneers"). In lines anticipating Jeffers' "The Torchbearers' Race" Whitman wrote in "Facing West From California's Shores"

Look off over the shores of my Western sea—
    the circle almost circled;
For starting Westward from Hindustan, from
    the vales of Kashmere,
From Asia— from the north— from the God,
    the sage, and the hero;
From the south— from the flowery peninsulas,
    and the spice islands,
Now I face the old home again— very pleas'd
    and joyous.…

But that "very pleas'd and joyous" sets him definitively apart from Jeffers and Lowell, though Whitman does see the disjunction between man and nature so accented in modern society, as well as the need to heal that split, if unaware of the Jeffersian nets even then being let out.

Nonetheless Whitman is not blind to American failings. He imagines helping an auctioneer sell a slave more effectively in "I Sing The Body Electric."

Gentlemen look on this curious creature,
Whatever the bids of the bidders they cannot be
    high enough for him,
For him the globe lay preparing quintillions of
    years without one animal or plant,
For him the revolving cycles truly and steadily
    rolled.
…
Who degrades or defiles the living human body
    is cursed.…

9. Inflation

All these poets get carried away by their out-sized ambition into megalomania, scolding egotism, and personal self-advertisement and obsession. They confuse their lyric 'I' with their autobiographical 'I' and for a time speak as if their underlying vision and the poetic persona that lets them communicate that vision are identical with their private ego, the mere, personal 'me' of any of us. From that moment the flood of Universal Soul, or the amoral God of Nature, or of (however diminished) Reality ceases, and instead we hear the dull repetition of 'me me me' or hysterical reproaches that seem personal and unbalanced.

This is an archetypal behavior, common enough in psychopathology where, say, a patient identifies with his hallucinations, and even more so in mythology. Joseph Campbell in an insight of great brilliance in *The Hero With A Thousand Faces* points out that the villain the hero overcomes in renewing life *is a fallen hero*, one who has become a giant of egotism and thinks the cosmic, creative power he wielded as a hero is his own. This giant egotism is the dark side of these poets' ambition.

Almost immediately after the first edition of *Leaves of Grass* Whitman proposes in his notes

> The Great Construction of the New Bible. Not
> to be diverted from the principal object— the
> main life work— the three hundred and sixty-
> five. It ought to be ready in 1859.

A "New Bible"... The number '365' refers to three hundred and sixty-five poems to be regarded as chapters or psalms. He is no longer the *poetic* Whitman persona bringing the news of universal human brotherhood and deathlessness through the constant rebirth of the soul, but now the actual

Walt Whitman demanding recognition as a giant among men, a New Bible bringer.

The degeneration of the lyric 'I' in Jeffers too lies at the root of the ill-temper and excesses his critics in the 1930s and 1940s gleefully threw back at him. His *inflation* isn't Whitman's megalomania but ill-disciplined runs to excess in his transports, first noted in the title poem of *The Women At Point Sur* in 1927, a disenchantment with the world around him that steadily deepened into a bitter personal pessimism as he anticipated the coming of World War II long before most other public figures.

Some of this angry personal tone replacing the Jeffersian lyric 'I' is seen in the concluding lines of "The Purse Seine."

> These things are Progress;
> Do you marvel our verse is troubled or
>   frowning, while it keeps its reason? Or lets
>   go, lets the mood flow
> In the manner of the recent young men into
>   mere hysteria, splintered gleams, crackled
>   laughter? But they are quite wrong.
> There is no reason for amazement: surely one
>   always knew that cultures decay, and life's
>   end is death.

"Our verse" here amounts to a claim of personal identification, and we wonder from the topical language just who are the "recent young men" who are hysterics? Jeffers' assumption of a lyric poet's right to speak of "our" when he means 'do you marvel *my* verse is troubled' gave an easy target to the hounds of envy, and in fact the New Critics began their assault on Jeffers about this time in the 1930s. Over time their impact was so great that Jeffers' reputation still has not fully recovered— on the American East Coast. We need to remind ourselves at times of the Emersonian insight, "Colleges hate genius, just as convents hate saints." Envy, the expression of our will to destroy, which is a deep part of human nature, flies out at any opportunity.

In the heyday moment of the *quantum leap* and *rapture* these poets are able to poke fun at themselves, whether Whitman with sidelong glances at his posturing, or sounding his "barbaric yawp", or Jeffers with his realization that seeps through the earlier great poems that the lives and visions he communicates are safely distanced from himself, even implying he is only an "ape of God" in one poem. Lowell writes of exhausting everyone with his turmoil. That distancing, that sense of measure, disappears in *inflation.*

Inflation for Lowell takes a turn both disastrous for himself and American poetry, for it is in the works after *For The Union Dead* that his lyric 'I' becomes a merely confessional 'me', and decades of self-indulgent confessions are unleashed parading as poems. Frank Bidart in his quixotic Introduction to Lowell's *Collected Poems* brings home the public perception of the post *For The Union Dead* poet.

When he published in 1973 three sonnet books— *The Dolphin, History,* and *For Lizzie and Harriet*— many reviewers were bewildered: two of these volumes came out of his previous book called *Notebook* (which Bidart consciously leaves out of the 'collected' poems). *The Times Literary Supplement*, in what we may characterize as an unsympathetic view of revision (!), ran a drawing of a meat grinder chewing up books with its review, its handle turned by a man who stares out at us demonically, with a half-smile. The man is, of course, Robert Lowell.

The vision of Lowell wandering about with the *Notebooks* manuscripts (*Notebook 1967-68,* published in 1969, and *Notebook,* published in 1970) with endless revisions is not reassuring, nor is Lowell's own remark about different versions of a poem, "But they both exist", nor Bidart's defense of revising which needs no defense, nor his justification of leaving undecided preferences between different versions of poems, as if *"That we need not choose"* is an acceptable principle of artistry. After

For The Union Dead the collapse of the lyric 'I' for Lowell brings with it a near-pathological inability to bring a poem to fruition, the ultimate instance of incoherence for an artist, a breakdown he can no longer make representative of society at large.

This point about *inflation* as it relates to the loss of the lyric 'I' is paradoxical.

Isn't the assertion of authenticity these poets make in their *quantum leap* and *rapture* what we want? Don't we want an authentic self to confront real experience and in all non-ironic sincerity make a judgment and stand behind it? We hunger for such men and women. But true authenticity does not lie that way we saw for a defining poet. He is a conduit of something larger than himself into his society that he hopes will lead to health and enlightenment, an eruption into mundane fact of the ideal meant by "human" however formulated by each poet. That communication is such a poet's authenticity, and can only be made within the lyric 'I'. *The insight of the defining poet does not belong to him: he is only its servant.* He brings it *for us.*

10. Return

The element of *return* most sets these defining voices apart from other poets. They recover their health when hope for that seems lost, and again they are able to reach out to the common man through a rediscovered, perhaps redefined lyric 'I'.

Whitman was never again the poet of the 1855 *Leaves of Grass*. Experience too often became something to be quarried for material for a new song, abstraction crept into his language, and various stylistic quirks became pronounced, whether his endless lists, or constant rewriting of the original *Leaves of Grass*, especially of "Song of Myself". The revisions betray his need to rationalize what once was instinctive and sufficient unto itself. The tendency to mine experience for material is a particular disaster, for it is the modern disease par excellence to be alienated from one's experience, and instead to treat it as an object to be used, like a shampoo, rather than the essence of experiencing oneself creatively alive and communicating that experience, as Whitman does so brilliantly in the 1855 "Song of Myself".

But the impact of nursing the wounded during the Civil War with his long recovery from the breakdown this caused deflated him so that his latent powers allowed him to give once more unquestioningly of himself. Now as the 'Good Gray Poet' he asserts a lyric 'I' that represents a new 'I/Thou':'

> A worship new I sing,
> You captains, voyagers, explorers, yours,
> You engineers, you architects, machinists, yours,
> You, not for trade or transportation only,
> But in God's name, and for thy sake O soul.
>   from "Passage to India"

Again Whitman is a conduit, now for the Universal Soul (God), the lyric 'I' of the chanting poet trying to bring our individual souls in touch with a universal Soul through a poem celebrating the civilizing of the entire globe, and the next onward phase of mankind, where "Nature and Man ... /...shall absolutely fuse...." And should the voyage stop there?

> O sun and moon and all you stars! Sirius and
>   Jupiter!
> Passage to you!
>   from "Passage to India"

Jeffers gives voice to the same theme of onward, upward ascendance and 'passage' in "The Torch-Bearers' Race", both literal continued passage and metaphysical passage to the indescribable cosmic, creative, nameless heart of the universe.

Having found out flight in the air to make
  wing to the height, fierce eye-flames
Of the eaglets be strengthened, to drink of the
  fountain of the beauty of the sun of the
  stars, and to gaze in his face, not a father's,
And motherless and terrible here.

Lowell shows too this regained sense of the soul's quest and his own limits in "Grass Fires" in his last book, *Day by Day*.

The fire-engines deployed with stage bravado,
yet it was I who put out the fire,
who slapped it to death with my scarred leather
  jacket.
I snuffed out the inextinguishable root,
I—
really I can do little...
...
about the infernal fires—
I cannot blow out a match.

He begins with the illusion of reality (confessional poetry), but realizes it is the use of memory that counts, and then tries to rewrite that as he recounts setting a fire trying to smoke out a rabbit. It blazes, and he snuffs it out himself, snuffing out the "inextinguishable root" now much more than a root of Grandfather's endangered tree, or an oedipal root, but the "inextinguishable root" *itself* in either a Jeffersian or Whitmanesque sense. He fails. That isn't how it happened. The inextinguishable root is beyond his power and, implicitly, ours. That failure brings him up tellingly against his all-too-human limitations, extending equally to his failure to control his madness ("infernal fires") or equally, implicitly, *his vision.* Again a lyric 'I/Thou' resonates here, his frailty combined with ours lifting us together to a true view of reality.

It is this recovery by Lowell in *Day by Day* which at once discomforted critics who after the preceding work were prepared to give him little credit despite the Pulitzer Prize he received for *The Dolphin*, yet which drew grudging admiration, too. Constantly he rises from the confessional 'me' to the true lyric 'I'. His verse is freer to free again, rhyme largely abandoned in any formulaic way, so we don't get the *ring-a-ling-a-ding* sort of nonsense he was capable of producing after abandoning all other traditional elements.

Jeffers makes the most encompassing recovery. He recovers his authentic voice in *The Double Axe* with its bitter World War Two anti-war sentiments, including the incredible disrobing moment in Part I as the returning son bares what should be his lethal wound but which his will has defied in order to come home to show the price of 'patriotism'. He tears off his tunic and bares his left side, black with wounds: one is like

> ...a wide grinning mouth, where a mortar shell fragment
> Had crushed in through two ribs...
> ...
> ...She whispered, "I believe.
> Have mercy on me." "Damn you, put in your hand."
> She came like a sleepwalker feeling her way,
> Wide sightless eyes, and laid her hand on the purulent
> Lips of the wound. He said, "Deeper," she slipped
> Her hand into the hollow...

This is not overkill as the New Critics would have it in their puerility, but a Dantesque ferocity over our failings, and pallid compared to the ovens at Auschwitz and the mentality that created them. A key difference between Dante and Jeffers is that Dante watches those suffering in *The Inferno* with a guide: with Jeffers, as with Lowell in his family drama, we are in the midst of the action.

Part II develops Jeffers' philosophy of "inhumanism". The first remedy is death; the second is to recognize that whatever we may do

> The mountains appear to be on their feet still.
> And down there the dark ocean nosing his
> bays and tide-breaks
> Like a bear in a pit. As for the human race, we
> could do without it; but it won't die.
> Oh: slightly scorched. It will slough its skin,
> and crawl forth
> Like a serpent in spring.

We will die, but those of us who can live within the larger picture of the whole of creation just may have a chance for balance and health that will find our wars and other excesses hideous and not try to make excuses for them, and so live beyond and despite them.

Finally, in "Beginnings and Ends", Jeffers comes almost directly to Whitman's vision in the original "Song of Myself", writing

> ... all things are conscious;
> But the nerves of an animal, the nerves and brain
> Bring it to focus...
> ... they feel and feed and in-
> fluence each other, each unto all,
> Like the cells of a man's body making one being,
> They make one being, one consciousness, one
> life, one
> God.

So many years have passed since Lowell's death in 1977. We have long been ready for and in need of a new defining voice, one that can again make our own language capable of communicating the wholeness of experience, its meaning, and our interrelatedness even to the very source of being where 'self' and 'other' are contained in one 'I/Thou'. None of this is magic. We are bound in a historical process that is also a spiritual movement, and the spirit's needs demand satisfaction even more powerfully than the body's. But the appearance of genius is an accident of birth, not of social need.

A poetry of such directness and ambition will have to break through a wall of indifference and challenge an entrenched critical unknowing, too. The poetry will seem anomalous, not of this time or another, although quintessentially of this time and speaking to us. In America this is a particularly difficult problem as so many and so much of American poets and poetry are associated with some University's English Department, understandable enough on a purely human level as a means to earn a living. But in this milieu one generation of critical zealots supplants another as each in turn gets tenure and resists change, their voices in turn frozen echoes of Levi-Straus, or Lacan, or Foucault, or Derrida and the rest, all suffering from the delusion their derivative criticism is somehow as important as an act of creation. Lowell never broke with the American University's traditional Euro-centrism, nor consistently from traditional modernist prosody, although it is only his reinvention of *our* common language that we retain. To the extent a poet belongs to an 'ism' or is an 'ist' he must sing in a minor key.

Worse, the University treats literature and contemporary poetry like geological extracts to be classified, used, negated, or approved as they fit one or another of these preexisting critical categories or usages, all overlaid with multiculturalism and, especially, with epidemic political correctness. It makes a mockery of Emerson's almost 180 year old remarks in *The American Scholar.*

> Public and private avarice make the air we
> breathe thick and fat

he begins. But the scholar is the man "delegated" to concentrate on "intellect", but that is inadequate, for

> in the right state he is *Man Thinking.* In the
> degenerate state, when the victim of society, he
> tends to become a mere thinker, or still worse,
> the parrot of other men's thinking.

Yet

> If there is any period one would desire to be
> born in, is it not the age of Revolution; when the
> old and the new stand side by side and admit
> of being compared; when the energies of all
> men are searched by fear and hope; when the
> historic glories of the old can be compensated
> by the rich possibilities of the new era? This
> time, like all times, is a very good one, if we but
> knew what to do with it.

The *timeliness* of these lines is depressing, like the contemporary failure of American literary critics to root themselves in our common experience of revolutionary transformation and to speak from this edge of native experience. The critical obsession with so often non-American models, the reduction of individual artists and their works to facets of classifiable experience, the cannibalization of art and experience, with an arcane style of writing as though preparing a legal brief carefully citing precedent to prove the writer is knowledgeable but not too innovative, wreathed in quotations, are, in the academic arena, a microcosm of the same incoherencies and insecurities characterizing modern post-industrial society where all is for sale and every self/fragment exploitable in its isolation from every other.

How our social media try to combat this, but provide only the illusion of 'friends' and connectedness in the virtual reality of the internet as opposed to the actual potency of immediate, shared experience. We reach out ever farther, and touch ever fewer.

The burden of one of these defining poets is to return us to the wholeness of experience, to remind us life is lived, not a raw material to be written about, and that language is to speak to one another of our needs; that man may be wonderful or awful, but is part of a larger order, and desperately needs both to know and to *feel* that to be healthy and overcome the violence which consumes self and society. Poetry works on the edge of the inexpressible to broaden and to redeem consciousness from both chaos and speechlessness and to reground our moral sense. It is a tall order, and no wonder that the poets who find themselves going down this path find it such a burden.

That fresh appearance of an American Voice will likely have to be Western, too, where the real creative, American edge exists today on the broad curve of the Pacific shore of the continent and its hinterland, whether indigenous or immigrant, permanent or passing. The real American Voice has the largesse of the West, and its wider, global, Pacific perspective. That voice, mind you, is as much a state of mind as place, although the two are related and the one cannot be had without some escape into the wider Western places of the American place and soul. Nor is that voice manifested only in poetry, as this concluding passage from Norman MacLean's *A River Runs Through It* shows. Norm, his elderly persona, reflects on how everything fades and there is just the sound of the river in the "Arctic half-light of the canyon" where he, his father, and tragic brother, once fished together. Now as he casts, alone, he imagines how the river's flow merges with

> ... a four-count rhythm and the hope that a fish will rise.
> Eventually, all things merge into one, and a river runs through it. The river was cut by the world's great flood and runs over the rocks from the basement of time. On some of the rocks are raindrops. Under the rocks are the words, and some of the words are theirs.
> I am haunted by waters.

The fusion of self with nature and of one with all, clearly stated and feelingly evoked, are typical of that voice. Under the surface American celebration of individuality lies a deeper sense of brotherhood stretching across time and place, and union with nature. We recognize that voice when it breaks through, its urgency, its human reek, and its size that matches our hunger for even the briefest moment to be whole and at one and at peace with the Other in the wider universe that so tolerantly endures us.

Portrait by John Robertson.

ABOUT THE AUTHOR

Lance Lee is a poet, playwright (*Time's Up and Other Plays*), novelist (*Second Chances*) and writer on drama and screenwriting (*A Poetics for Screenwriters*, and *The Death and Life of Drama*). His six previous volumes of poetry are listed under "Previous Books". *Seasons of Defiance* was a 2010 USA National Best Books Award finalist. *Transformations* (2013) uniquely combines art and poetry with the collaboration of a number of noted artists. His poems appear widely in America and England, between which his family is split. A past Creative Writing Fellow of the National Endowment for the Arts, his home is in Los Angeles, where he has also taught at a number of leading universities. Also an environmentalist, he was instrumental in forming the California State Park system in the Santa Monica Mountains.

Lightning Source UK Ltd.
Milton Keynes UK
UKHW021328231120
373748UK00019B/454

9 781532 098291